Character Disorders in Parents of Delinquents

Beatrice Simcox Reiner
Irving Kaufman, M.D.

FAMILY SERVICE ASSOCIATION OF AMERICA
44 East Twenty-Third Street   New York, N. Y. 10010

Library of Congress Catalog Number: 59-15631

ISBN: 0-87304-089-9

Printed in the U.S.A.

3

Contents

CONTENTS

Index of Cases

Introduction

No ONE DOUBTS that treatment of juvenile delinquents is far more likely to be successful if the parents are included in the treatment process. However, little has been written about the psychological dynamics of these adults or about the techniques of treating them. It has frequently been noted that the parents of delinquents have strong resistance to becoming involved in agency contact, and that they often carry a heavy emotional burden because of their own inner conflicts, their sense of failure, and the overwhelming economic and social problems with which many are confronted.

It is our belief that part of the difficulty that social workers and psychiatrists have encountered in working with parents of delinquents is related to the type of pathology these individuals present. In the main, therapeutic methods in clinics and social agencies are geared to the treatment of persons who have achieved a sufficiently high level of personality development to be motivated to seek help and to engage in a treatment relationship. It is becoming increasingly clear that a large number of parents of delinquents have not reached this level of maturation and, therefore, do not respond to conventional methods.

We found, in classifying the cases studied in the juvenile delinquency research unit of the Judge Baker Guidance Center, that a majority of the parents fell into the category of impulse-ridden character disorders. It seems likely that a relatively high proportion of adults under the care of other agencies also belong in this category. The proportion is doubtless highest in agencies dealing with delinquents and "hard-to-reach" families, but a considerable number are also to be found in the caseloads of agencies providing child and family services, health care, public assistance, and so forth. Clients with character disorders present difficult and perplexing problems to all these agencies, not only because these clients are numerically frequent but because they display such an extreme degree of social pathology in all their family and community rela-

3

tionships. It is probably safe to say that families with members suffering from severe character disorders represent the most serious social problem in our country.

In financial terms, these families account for a large part of current expenditures for public assistance, police departments, correctional systems, mental hospitals, child placement facilities, and various other institutional and welfare programs. In human terms, as well, the cost of this type of psychological disorder is extremely high. The parents of these families are not only the "marginal workers" described by economists, but they are "marginal" human beings in the sense that they live on the edge of life. They are vulnerable to every wind that blows—economic, social, and physical. A child born into such a family has a negligible chance of growing into a normal, healthy, and useful adult. Although the parents may often appear to be selfish and pleasure-loving, they live their lives in the shadow of failure, defeat, and rejection. It is this paradoxical combination of pleasure-seeking and misery that often confounds the better organized persons who try to help them, as well as the public generally. Most people see only the hedonistic behavior and its results and are unaware of the misery that the behavior conceals. Fiction often portrays this paradox more graphically than does the social work literature. One recent novel on the best seller list, Nelson Algren's *A Walk on the Wild Side*, is a good example.

Our purpose in this volume is to focus attention on the impulse-ridden character disorder as a psychological entity. We have endeavored to describe the dynamics of this disorder and to outline treatment techniques that take into account these dynamics. We realize, of course, that not all parents of delinquents fall into this category. We also recognize that, by limiting our discussion to the clinical aspects of delinquency, we are omitting other equally important aspects—the socio-economic, legal, moral, and so on.

The seeming inconsistency of the behavior of persons who have character disorders has been a source of confusion to clinicians and has made classification of these cases difficult. It seems to us that the only sound classification that can be made is in relation to the person's primary pregenital level of fixation which determines his defenses. Recognition of this dynamic base provides a means for

4

making a meaningful classification and for analyzing behavior that otherwise seems random and unrelated. In two earlier articles,[1] we presented a formulation for such classification, and identified the oral and anal types of character disorder. In the present formulation, we have added a third category—the phallic-urethral character. We recognize and regret that there is a certain awkwardness in these descriptive phrases. We do not like to classify people in dehumanizing terms but we believe that it is necessary to have some way of grouping them in order to understand them. The use of less scientific terms would incur the risk of their becoming "tags" that might be used in a way to discredit a group of people who need sympathetic understanding.

Classification in itself is useless unless it leads to better understanding of the client and to improved methods of treatment. We believe that, through our detailed analysis of various types of character disorders, we have been able to suggest a general treatment approach and also to outline appropriate techniques for clients at different levels of development. We do not think we are claiming too much if we say that the treatment method outlined here fills one of the major gaps in the spectrum of psychotherapy.

Casework, as one form of psychotherapy, has its own place in this spectrum. We believe that the treatment of persons with character disorders is a particularly suitable function for casework practitioners for several reasons: (1) persons with character disorders, who rarely seek treatment for their inner stresses voluntarily, come to the attention of social agencies because of their social or environmental problems; (2) social agencies are in a position to search out such persons or families in the interest of prevention; and (3) treatment methods require a combination of psychological and environmental techniques. In other words, the social agency caseworker has access to these clients and can best adapt his therapeutic methods to meet their needs.

In describing the classifications and outlining the various stages of treatment, we inevitably have had to generalize. However, we have

[1] Beatrice R. Simcox and Irving Kaufman, M.D., "Treatment of Character Disorders in Parents of Delinquents," *Social Casework*, Vol. XXXVII, No. 8 (1956), pp. 388–395.

Beatrice R. Simcox and Irving Kaufman, M.D., "Handling of Early Contacts with Parents of Delinquents," *Social Casework*, Vol. XXXVII, No. 9 (1956), pp. 443–450.

tried to convey the idea that we are thinking of "people" rather than "cases." We should like to stress that, although a client may show behavior characteristic of a particular stage of development, he will have his own individual differences. Also, the techniques described should not be applied too literally. The treatment approach should be geared to the client's dynamics but, in carrying forward the treatment, the caseworker should be guided by his intuition. He can be helpful to his clients only if he responds to them as people.

It is pertinent to describe briefly our research plan. During a five-year period, the delinquency research unit undertook to study thoroughly the actual treatment of a small group of cases with which each member of the unit could be familiar. This plan seemed more appropriate for our purposes than a survey type of research which would be based largely on examination of the recorded material of other therapists. The primary objective was to provide help for the clients; at no time were procedures introduced merely for reasons of facilitating the research. Frequent conferences were held by the therapists treating a particular family and also by the unit as a whole. These staff conferences made it possible for all participants to be kept up to date with case problems as they emerged and also with the treatment. One of our most important findings was that the therapists who handled these cases required emotional support from each other.

We are indebted to the Judge Baker Guidance Center and to the Family Service Association of Greater Boston for permission to use case material. (All case material has been disguised.) In addition, we wish to express our gratitude to other members, past and present, of the delinquency research unit of the Judge Baker Guidance Center for their emotional support and intellectual stimulus during this study, and especially to Lora Heims, Ph.D., Joan Zilbach, M.D., David Reiser, M.D., and Chester C. d'Autremont, M.D.

We wish to acknowledge appreciation to the National Institute of Mental Health, U. S. Public Health Service, for a research grant (M826) to conduct this investigation.

BEATRICE SIMCOX REINER
IRVING KAUFMAN, M.D.

November 10, 1959

I. The Impulse-ridden Adult Client

So MUCH CONFUSION surrounds the concept of character disorder at the present time that we should at the outset define the group that is the subject of this presentation. The parents of delinquents whom we shall discuss are persons suffering from character disorders who are fixated at pregenital levels of development and who express their conflicts primarily by behavioral manifestations that are based on characteristics associated with the oral, anal, and phallic-urethral stages of development. It is important to distinguish these persons from those with other types of characterological disturbance, such as the hysterical or the schizoid type. The behavior associated with persons with character disorders may include stealing, getting pregnant, creating job difficulties, or becoming involved in social crises. They operate at such an infantile level that they defeat themselves in nearly all aspects of life. Although some may have partial control, they usually are so impulse-ridden that they tend to pursue the wrong ends or the right ends at the wrong time. Such persons have often been placed in catch-all categories like "psychopathic personality" or "constitutional psychopath" by clinicians, and there has been a tendency to regard their disturbance as untreatable. This concept has seemed at variance with the dynamic theory of behavior, but the group has been difficult to study and treat.

Basically, persons with character disorders are constantly threatened by the anxiety stemming from an unresolved depression. Much of their activity is designed to ward off the anxiety. They attempt to deal with it by acting-out behavior or by developing physical symptoms. They may outwardly display excessive calm, but inwardly they are seething and supersensitive. They have only a small repertory of behavior patterns to which they adhere rigidly. To the inexperienced observer, these patterns may appear varied and unpredictable because they differ from accepted norms and because the motivation for such behavior is often obscure.

The truth of the matter is that these people do not distinguish among various types of emotional tension and, as a result, any kind of emotional drive, whether affect hunger or hostility, precipitates the same response. One deprived mother, for instance, always reacted to hostile treatment from her mother-in-law by telephoning the caseworker to announce that her daughter would not be allowed to attend the club that was part of the therapy. After she had been encouraged to tell the whole story and had received some comfort and reassurance, she would withdraw her prohibition. Her retaliation, directed toward the clinic instead of the mother-in-law, revealed her inability to distinguish between sources of pain and tension. Another example of undifferentiated response may be found in the sadistic courting behavior of some teenage delinquents. One girl patient, who had been making aggressive overtures to a boy patient, responded to a sudden slap from him as if it were proof that he reciprocated her tender feelings.

These impulse-ridden people appear to be in a perpetual state of crisis. It is not so much that they enjoy the uncertainty and chaos, as that they must have "something happening" in order to feel alive. The caseworker or other persons who try to help them often wonder how these clients can survive so much turmoil. It is useless, however, to postpone working with these families until the situation settles down, because this never happens. One must relate to these clients in the midst of their crises, or not at all. A further difficulty is that these acting-out persons—in spite of the intensity of their emotions—cannot enter into a discussion of their feelings and behavior. Their way of communicating is through actions.

Such activity is in contrast with the symbolic symptom formation and the affective or somatic reactions of psychotic and neurotic patients. It must be remembered, however, that the symptom complexes are not mutually exclusive; they represent different methods employed by the ego to cope with conflicts.

The Stage of Development

The diagnosis of character disorders is made difficult by the diversity of personality characteristics found in these impulse-ridden persons. We have found it useful and meaningful to classify them according to the cluster of overt and manifest personality traits which are most specifically associated with a given level of psychosexual development. In an effort to make the criteria for classification as objective as possible, we have focused on such data as symptoms, dress, nature of object relationships, and attitudes.

In reviewing our cases, we found that none of the parents had reached the oedipal level of development. Instead, they demonstrated clusters of personality traits typical of the characterological manifestations of the pregenital stages of development, that is, the oral-erotic, oral-sadistic, anal-erotic, anal-sadistic, and phallic-urethral. Although none of our cases was fixated primarily at the phallic-urethral level of development, a number of characteristics of this phase were present in the "mixed" types. Our findings of the group studied at the clinic are borne out by our experience with similar clients in other settings. In subsequent chapters, we shall describe in some detail the personality characteristics associated with each of these stages of development and their relation to difficulties in the treatment process. At this point, however, it may be useful to review in a more general way some considerations related to these personality types.

Since these clients have not resolved their oedipal conflicts, they inevitably have major problems in respect to object relationships, concepts of identity, and thought processes. Infantile object relationships are manifested in several ways. For example, these clients tend to view all persons as potential giving or depriving parents or they may try to force people to control or care for them by creating crises. Male and female identities are viewed by them in terms of symbolic or stereotyped phenomena rather than on a biologic basis; they often associate activity, sadism, power, and independence with a male identity, and masochism, helplessness, and dependency with a female identity. Since they desire both male and female attributes, they frequently act out a particular attribute with the hope of magically accomplishing a particular end. If they wish to be cared for and be in a dependent role, they may develop illnesses, incur an injury, or utilize some other masochistic pattern. If they have a need to be independent or acquisitive, they are likely to react aggressively or sadistically. Because so much of their behavior is associated with living out or acting out these role concepts, it is important not to take the illness, masochistic activity, or sadism at face value. These manifestations should ultimately be related to their concept of identity.

Since the superego, as a definite part of the personality structure, develops only with the resolution of the oedipal conflict, none of these patients has an adequately evolved superego. What are sometimes identified as manifestations of the superego are, in reality, a group of ego functions, such as mechanisms of identification, repetition compulsion, and so forth. This point, as well as points about identity, will be discussed in greater detail in later chapters.

Typical Features

Study of persons with character disorders reveals certain typical features: a history of traumatic episodes, major disturbance in psychosexual development, and a characteristic pattern of ego pathology. The trauma often includes the actual or emotional loss of parents. In our cases, the adult clients reacted as if they had been abandoned by their parents—even though the latter might be dead—and were searching for them. They seemed angry at the loss and did not, as a general rule, show the usual affective reaction. Instead, they denied the feeling of loss while attempting to deal with it in various substitutive ways. We found no overt depression in our cases, but rather a process of denial and a resultant core of anxiety which we called a "depressive nucleus." [1] The characteristic pathological ego mechanisms which these clients manifested at the time of initial contact were those of denial, displacement, projection, and the repetitive compulsion of antisocial acting out. They denied the affective component of the loss of parents and dis-

---

[1] Irving Kaufman, M.D., "Three Basic Sources for Pre-delinquent Character," *The Nervous Child*, Vol. XI, No. 1 (1955), pp. 12–15.

placed the anxiety onto other persons—the landlord, school teacher, or neighbor. In the displacement, they often became involved in intense situations, in which all family members took part. Some tried to narcotize the hurt by alcohol, promiscuity, or hyperactivity. The pathology included stealing and desertion. It would seem that the specific choice of symptom depends upon a variety of factors, including especially the level of psychosexual fixations and the client's particular identifications. These factors will be elaborated later in discussion of the clinical subgroups.

Dynamics of Treatment

Persons with character disorders are likely to show evidences of personality reorganization during the treatment process, but one must be aware of the forms that these are likely to take. As in any treatment of personality, the medium through which reorganization takes place is the relationship. The process of forming a relationship with this group of clients is often a long and complicated one, but if it can be accomplished, the stage is set for further growth. The client's resistance to forming a close relationship is twofold: (1) he fears that the caseworker will not see him through the turmoil he anticipates, and (2) he fears an increase in the depression and anxiety that he is always trying to ward off. For a long time, there is a back and forth movement—advancing and retreating. Eventually, however, these clients will incorporate enough of the caseworker's ego strength to give them sufficient courage to face their depressive nucleus.

Certain typical features are associated with this early phase of treatment if it moves forward. The client, instead of taking recourse to flight and denial, will gradually begin to communicate his feeling of hurt. The hurt may be expressed in physical and psychosomatic symptoms or in the client's sudden concern about neglected teeth, obesity, menstrual irregularities, and so forth. The affect associated with the physical component frequently provides an opening for a discussion of the psychological hurt. The feeling about the physical disorder is often expressed as, "Why does this have to happen to me?" The question can lead to a discussion of his feelings of psychological neglect, of feeling unloved and devalued. In this phase of treatment, the client requires considerable support

11

from the caseworker. In the course of facing his sense of loss, the client through identification incorporates the attitudes of the caseworker and evolves a new ego-ideal and sense of identity. He then proceeds to test his new identity with the caseworker.

With the resolution of the affective depression, the client's ego has at its disposal the psychic energy that previously was caught up in the process of denial, flight, projection, and the repetitive acting out of antisocial behavior. The ego reorganization and the new level of object identity provides him with the energy needed to work on the problems related to the phallic-urethral-oedipal stage of development. In many ways this later phase of treatment is analogous to the treatment of adolescents; both types of client must deal with the oedipal struggle as well as with the unresolved fragments of the pregenital stages of development. Both also are struggling with problems related to masturbation, homosexuality, and promiscuity. They alternate between love and hate for the mother and father figures, and convey their fears of acting out the equivalent of an incest relationship with the parent of the opposite sex, or of a homosexual relationship with the parent of the same sex. The advance in personality growth through treatment, of both the adolescent and the adult with a character disturbance, makes such acting out less probable but increases anxiety and phobic expressions of the unresolved conflict.

Treatment, during this oedipal stage, includes focusing on the client's achievement, competition, and male-female identity problems associated with the phallic-urethral stage. The resurgence of homosexual problems should be dealt with in the context of resolving the identity problems. The emergence of sexual acting-out behavior, or of conflicts about pregenital sexual problems, can set a trap for the therapist. He may be tempted to view any of these manifestations as separate entities, instead of seeing them as part of the stage of development which the client is trying to master. The manifestations are the client's way of communicating his struggle with these developmental problems. His search for identity often manifests itself in the treatment relationship in a libidinized form, which can be threatening to both the patient and the therapist. The defenses associated with this phase of treatment are either hostility or flight. However, if the therapist is aware of the meaning of

12

the reactions, they too can be handled. The client, at this stage of treatment, is dealing with the resolution of the oedipal struggle, which brings him nearer to the neurotic level of development. Until he resolves the conflict, he cannot achieve a sense of personal identity.

When this reorganization of the ego structure takes place, the individual is able to make reality choices about things which, until now, he has been handling in an unreal way. He becomes better able to handle his work and his relationships with parents, children, and his marital partner, on an objective basis. Prior to this time, attempts to help the client direct his energies into more socially acceptable channels usually fail, since there can be no sublimation of pregenital impulses until the genital stage is reached.[2]

The residual scars of the early traumatic experiences of these patients are now dealt with by neurotic mechanisms. We have found that the higher level of functioning is characterized primarily by the use of obsessive compulsive mechanisms. The result is a certain rigidity in personality, but there is far less crippling of functioning than that which operated in the previous severe characterological disorder. Achieving this compulsive level of functioning may well represent the maximum therapeutic goal toward which treatment may be geared.

A recognition of the immature and pathological ego development of these clients [3] and of the dynamic process by which improvement may be effected makes it clear that short-term therapy can do little for them. A few interviews are not sufficient to advance the necessary maturation process. In an earlier paper we referred to four stages of treatment as follows: (1) establishing a relationship, (2) identification with the caseworker, (3) separation from the caseworker, and (4) the client's understanding of his own behavior and its roots in the past.[4] In view of our increased knowledge of the process which takes place in the third stage, it might better be

[2] Otto Fenichel, M.D., *The Psychoanalytic Theory of Neurosis,* W. W. Norton and Co., New York, 1945, p. 141.

[3] Jurgen Ruesch, M.D., "The Infantile Personality: The Core Problem of Psychosomatic Medicine," *Psychosomatic Medicine,* Vol. X, No. 3 (1948), pp. 134–144.

[4] Beatrice R. Simcox and Irving Kaufman, M.D., "Treatment of Character Disorders in Parents of Delinquents," *Social Casework,* Vol. XXXVII, No. 8 (1956), pp. 388–395.

13

described as "establishing identity." We shall describe the four successive stages of treatment in subsequent chapters and point to the changes that occur in the client.

Who Should Be the Therapist?

In the above discussion of treatment of persons with character disorders, we have purposely not differentiated between psychiatrists and caseworkers as therapists. In most instances, such clients are seen by caseworkers because the nature of their problems brings them to the attention of social agencies. However, in some social agency settings, or in private practice, psychiatrists may deal with these cases. The dynamics of treatment are necessarily the same, regardless of the training of the therapist. In the long run, the efficacy of the treatment depends on the knowledge, skill, and patience of the person undertaking this demanding educational and therapeutic task. It is our belief that caseworkers have the necessary knowledge and skill to undertake such treatment, since the central aim is not to resolve unconscious conflicts but to further the maturation process.

Working with clients who have severe character disorders calls for special personal qualifications on the part of the caseworker. He must be able to tolerate the tremendous demands that these emotionally needful people make on him. He must be patient and able to curb his own anxiety and resentment and, at the same time, be constantly aware of his own reactions and feelings. Suppression or denial of feelings will interfere with the fluidity of communication with these clients. It is essential for the caseworker to be able to communicate both verbally and in a nonverbal symbolic way with these acting-out persons if treatment is to be successful. Such communication requires intuition, supplemented by technical knowledge about the meaning of behavior; neither one gets far without the other. The more understanding the caseworker has of his own reactions and those of the client, the better able he will be to use himself with flexibility in forming and maintaining a therapeutic relationship. He must be warm without being seductive, firm without being punitive, and accepting of the client's feelings without having to identify with his modes of behavior.

14

Etiological Factors

Understanding the pregenital character structure of the parents of delinquent children can also throw light on the etiology of the child's behavior. The utilization of delinquent mechanisms by the parents may be the result of many factors, including an unresolved depression due to their own loss of parental love, the sado-masochistic nature of their object relationships, and the pregenital libidinal fixations that demand immediate gratification.[5] Such parents have a tendency to subject their own children to similar losses and to experiences that will engender the same attitudes. It is important to recognize that the withdrawal of parental love in some cases may have been the result of the parent's actual death or desertion, or it may have resulted from physical neglect by the parent or from his acute depression or physical illness. Having experienced loss of love or inconsistent care themselves, they are unable as adults to provide a mature and consistent type of parental care for their children, but pass on these elements to them. Their relationship to their children, like their other relationships, is sado-masochistic in nature. Their own pregenital fixations, together with faulty ego development, make it difficult if not impossible for these parents to help their children to deal with their own pregenital impulses.

It is frequently said that the delinquent child acts out the unconscious wishes of the parent. Since the dynamics of this phenomenon are rarely explained, the caseworker must "take it or leave it" on a theoretical basis. If the caseworker takes the statement too literally, it can interfere seriously with his forming a relationship with the parent, since it suggests that the parent is actively working to corrupt the child. If, on the other hand, he dismisses the theory, he loses a chance to understand one of the important but subtle influences that are brought to bear on the child.

The evidence for supporting the theory is not hard to find. Often a parent himself engages in overt delinquencies or shows defiant attitudes that are counterparts of the child's behavior. But even in such cases, when the child gets in conflict with the law, the parent is enraged at the child's behavior. He does not condone the delinquency in the child or really condone it in himself. In some

---

[5] Irving Kaufman, M.D., *op. cit.*

15

instances, one form of delinquency may be acceptable to the parent while another form is nonacceptable. In these cases, we may find that the parent has led the child in a particular direction by his prohibitions. The parent is afraid that his own impulses, against which he has built a rigid reaction formation, will break through and he projects the danger onto the child. As a result, he conveys to the child the idea that the child will steal, become pregnant, or kill someone. Even the fear of killing is closer to the surface in many parents of delinquents than one would expect. After there has been publicity about some particularly brutal juvenile crime, the mother of a relatively mild delinquent may express fear that her child may become guilty of some such act. The parent's underlying feeling that the child is violent or crazy is obviously transmitted to the child in some way. Children in therapy often give expression to material that bears out this assumption.

Parents sometimes express a delinquent wish or attitude in some partial or vestigial way. One mother, who expressed horror at her son's stealing and truanting, showed pleasure in his defiant attitude toward a sarcastic woman teacher. However, when he was in danger of suspension from school, the mother became desperate in her efforts to make him conform. Another rather controlling mother hinted that she had another side to her nature when she said with real warmth that she loved children most at the age of two when "they go everywhere and investigate everything." This same mother had a daughter who was a persistent runaway, but it was not until we had known the mother for several years that it became apparent that when tensions mounted unbearably her own solution was to "walk out," and that this had been the pattern of her mother before her. In the third year of treatment, this same mother began to reveal the secret fascination that promiscuity held for her, and her fantasy of becoming promiscuous as a means of revenge against her depriving husband and mother. Still another mother, who deplored her son's flouting of the mores of the conservative suburb in which they lived, revealed her own ambivalence when she referred casually to the "stuffy attitudes" of the neighbors.

Under the surface of apparent conformity and "goodness" one frequently finds in a parent the need for some member of the family to be delinquent. A mother who grew up in a household with an aggressive or delinquent brother or father often needs to recreate the situation in her own household. She can be the good, conforming person only if someone else is acting the opposite role. When such a mother has two sons or two daughters, one often finds a kind of seesaw relationship between the siblings—when one is up (in favor with mother), the other is down. When the bad one turns good, the good one has to be bad. Thus, one can see various ways in which the parent's unconscious wishes prompt the delinquent behavior of the child. As a final example, there was the mother whose son was excluded from nursery school because he could not adjust to the other children. At this time, her husband was hospitalized and she reacted to it as desertion since it recreated her earlier losses. She complained bitterly to the caseworker that her siblings did not care what became of her, that the neighbors were unfriendly, and that the children in the housing project tormented her small son. One day, while the caseworker was visiting, there was a sound of crying outside and the mother suddenly threw open the window and with shouts and threats incited her son to beat up a smaller child.

We do not want to overemphasize the importance of the parents' delinquent wishes in the causality of juvenile delinquency. We wish only to explain it, since the relationship is frequently misunderstood. One should guard against the rationalization of the individual client who says, "This is what they expected of me, therefore this is what I am." He is using this theory as resistance against dealing with the problem within himself. Also, we should like to note that the loss of parents, the lack of a consistent parental figure with whom to identify, or the repetitive interruption of meaningful parent-child relationships can produce the same personality difficulties and the same types of delinquent behavior that we find in cases where the child's parents unconsciously wished him to be delinquent.

Summary

Persons with character disorders are fixated at pregenital levels of development. They express their conflicts and needs in behavior associated with one or more of these stages and they exhibit such behavior in response to almost any form of emotional tension.

Their underlying problem is anxiety which stems from an unre-solved depression. In treatment, the client's resistance to forming a close relationship with the caseworker must first be patiently overcome; he can then be helped to further maturation by tech-niques designed to help him incorporate ego strength, face his depressive nucleus, and evolve a sense of identity. In order to achieve this therapeutic goal, the caseworker must have adequate theoretical knowledge of the dynamics of behavior, as well as sound intuition and ability to communicate on verbal and nonverbal levels. If the caseworker understands the character structure of the parent of a delinquent, not only can he be of help to the parent but he often gains a clearer understanding of the dynamics of the delinquent himself.

II. The Oral Character Disorder

As A GROUP, persons with character disorders who are primarily fixated at the oral level of psychosexual development present a well-defined and consistent picture. These are people who suffered loss or trauma at the oral stage. The unsolved problems of orality overshadow any partial adaptation they have made to other stages of psychosexual development. In other words, as they aged chronologically they went through some phases of later development but the ultimate meaning of almost all experiences continues to be orally colored.

There are two types of character disorder of a primarily oral nature: the oral-erotic and the oral-sadistic. Genetically, the oral-erotic persons received substantial gratification and stimulation (along with deprivation) from a mother or mother substitute, which was followed by the trauma of a loss during the oral stage of infancy. The oral-sadistic persons experienced deprivation primarily. The former are the "sucking" type who have an expectation of receiving care and attention and the latter are the "biting" type who expect sadistic treatment. The trauma may have been the actual loss of the mother through death or desertion or an equivalent loss, such as the withdrawal of attention because the mother was ill or depressed. It may also have been a chronic kind of inconsistent maternal care. The latter is often seen in immature mothers who overstimulate a baby at one time and neglect him at another. The neglect is seen in the way such a mother holds or feeds her baby, giving him little support or comfort and not recognizing his needs.[1]

Oral characteristics permeate all aspects of the lives of both oral-erotic and oral-sadistic persons. They are impatient for gratification and cling desperately to any individual who may be a source of support. They function at a nonverbal level; to them, seeing, doing, and experiencing is the avenue to believing. Although they are often bright and have considerable verbal capacity, they are nonetheless at the mercy of their impulses and find themselves doing things that they did not intend to do. They establish an incorporative type of relationship with others, since they have not yet succeeded in separating the self from the non-self. This process of differentiation is part of the oral stage of infancy and begins when the child recognizes the mother as separate from him, when he begins to regard her as something more than a source of food. If the process of differentiation is not completed, the child makes any close relationship incorporative and continues to confuse identities and to have a distorted perception of reality.

An example of such confusion of identities is the oral-erotic mother who regards her children as part of herself. She makes a close-knit group of her family for the main purpose of meeting its members' mutual needs for mothering. The children meet the mother's needs and vice versa; they live together as in a nest. Inquiries about sleeping arrangements result in a confused account, since there is usually great competition about who will share the mother's bed. The lack of separation is emotional as well as physical. The mother tells the children all of her adult problems, whether they involve sex, money, feuds with the neighbors, or fear of dying. The family members tend to go on outings and expeditions together, and when one has an appointment they all turn up. The children are often excessively generous, sharing their candy with everyone. These children are apt to be pleasant company, since they have an awareness of the moods of adults and a wish to please. People tend to think of them as more mature than they really are and then to reject them when they "act up." They appear worldly wise but, in reality, they have an emotionally immature character structure. One of the real threats to the members of such a family is separation. The mother may

[1] Sylvia Brody, Ph.D., *Patterns of Mothering,* International Universities Press, New York, 1956.

request placement of the children during a period of discouragement, but quickly change her mind.

The social relationships of orally fixated people are never smooth. They vacillate between periods of almost complete withdrawal (when they are depressed but restrain themselves from acting out or expressing their dangerous anger) and intense relationships with people who serve as substitute parents or who are more childish and needy than they, and thus can give them vicarious pleasure through being the object of their feeding and comfort. They have no casual relationships; they absorb and incorporate people or they leave them alone. The oral person quickly wears out the parental substitute with his excessive dependency demands, which serve the double purpose of expressing his insatiable needs and of provoking rejection and abandonment.

One oral-erotic mother, Mrs. Hart, who was seen in a family service agency for many years, was extremely adept at enlisting the interest and help of people whom she met at church, at the medical clinic, or even on the bus. She had the characteristic ability to describe feelings which are repressed by people who have reached more mature levels of development, and to evoke a sympathetic response. Since she was obviously bright, her many reality problems seemed capable of solution. Many of the interested people gave tremendous amounts of time, effort, and money until it became evident that Mrs. H's ego strength was far below her verbal ability. They usually retreated from the situation with a burst of hostility, leaving Mrs. H again feeling like a rejected and abandoned infant. Mrs. H, too, took on less fortunate people, but ended these relationships as soon as the dependent ones showed signs of independence or criticized her.

The oral person perceives only two kinds of people—those who are for him (that is, part of him) and those who are against him (that is, outside him). In other words, the oral person can relate only by "swallowing up" or "spitting out" the other person. These are the basic oral mechanisms of introjection and projection.

It is difficult for the average person who has moved beyond the oral stage to comprehend the pervasiveness of the orality and the nature of the incorporative process. Novelists often can better convey nuances of feeling than can clinicians. Joyce Cary gives a clear picture of an oral reaction in Sara Monday, when Gulley Jimson, the ne'er-do-well artist with whom she previously had had an affair, paid her a visit.

> Talk away, I thought, but I won't ask you to tea. I'll give you no encouragement. But he went on talking about his great chance and the hole in his coat kept catching my eye until I said to him as coldly as a stranger: "Excuse me, but your coat seam is ripped."
>
> "Oh yes," he said, "it's been like that for a long time," and he started again on his wall and his travels. So I said to myself, if you will ruin a good coat, you will, and nothing can stop you. Wives or coats, you're a born waster. But the coat kept nagging at me. It was opening its mouth like a baby crying to be taken up and at last I could not bear it and I said: "Mr. Jimson, for poor Nina's sake, let me sew up your coat." [2]

To an anal person a rip in the coat would appear as something untidy that must be cleaned up but to Sara it was a hungry baby. Underlying the symbolism was her need to feed the hungry and neglected Gulley Jimson as a vicarious way of being fed and cared for herself.

Years later Sara and the artist have another conversation, this one reported by Gulley Jimson in *The Horse's Mouth.*

> "Is there anything you care about in this world except yourself?" I said, for I was growing exasperated.
>
> "Oh, Gulley, how can you ask? I was a true wife to you, and a true mother to your Tommy." "I was yourself, and so was Tommy. I was your best bed-warmer and Tommy was your heart cordial." "I nearly died when you left me." "Yes, as if you'd lost your left leg or your front teeth." [3]

The Oral-erotic Personality

Oral-erotic persons—those who as infants experienced oral overstimulation followed by loss—are always seeking to re-experience the original pattern (including both the excess and the deprivation). This repetition compulsion, expressed in a search for the lost mother, is the most important motive in their lives. Even the choice of the mate is based on the wish to mother and be mothered. Such men and women tend to choose mates with character structures similar to their own—those who have not established their own identities and whose problems make them unreliable. However, if a person gets even partial maternal gratification from a wife or

[2] Joyce Cary, *Herself Surprised,* Harper and Brothers, New York, 1941, p. 91.
[3] Joyce Cary, *The Horse's Mouth,* Harper and Brothers, New York, 1944, p. 183.

husband, it may not satisfy the need for mothering but only stir a desire for more. The person then attempts to satisfy these needs in some other way.

These emotionally starved people attempt to fill their emptiness by means of food, liquor, money, and sex. The compensatory eating may take the form of constant nibbling or occasional gorging. These persons often assert that they cannot understand their obesity, since they eat scarcely anything. Medically they frequently have severe deficiencies along with the obesity, since they fail to eat balanced meals but fill up with sweets and starches. Attempts to get such a person to diet are useless until some of the intensity of the emotional need has been reduced.

The drinking of oral-erotic persons differs from that of some other types of alcoholics. In fact, it often escapes diagnosis as alcoholism because, on the surface, it does not appear to have the compulsive qualities of an addiction; it seems rather to be a reaction to the person's depressed and empty feelings. These people can often find substitute forms of gratification. Alcoholics Anonymous is frequently successful with a drinker of this type, if he continues with the group long enough to feel the warmth and support of its members and to respond to the parental authority implicit in the religious emphasis.

Finances present notorious difficulties to people with oral-erotic character disorders. Since the wish of the moment cannot be postponed and there is always the hope that "things" will make them feel better, they are usually pursued by creditors and are frequently short of money before payday. Their homes reveal their impulsive buying. In a poorly furnished house or apartment, perhaps without enough chairs for everyone to sit on, there will be an expensive TV set, an electric mixer, and a pop-up toaster. One wóman, in an excess of generosity, decided to make a gift of a toaster (on time payments) to a neighbor who had cared for her during an illness. Unfortunately, the donor left town shortly after making the gift, leaving the friend with an unwelcome bill. When oral-erotic people get some money, they must dispose of it quickly. They seem to be unable to tolerate having resources.

To a person with an oral character disorder, sex represents primarily a search for closeness. It is not uncommon for the women to complain of frigidity, even though they give the outward appearance of a complete lack of sexual repression. They are seeking for the closeness of the mother holding the baby in her arms. They have a wish for skin sensation, which they perceive as an incorporative process of filling their emptiness; the sexual excitement of the man may make them feel alive. Frequently the demand for closeness by an oral-erotic person leads the partner, with similar personality, to start a fight in order to prevent being "swallowed up." Even though oral-erotic persons basically crave affection, they are afraid of it, because of its ultimate meaning. The oral triad means: to eat (or be eaten), to sleep, and to die (or kill). Since closeness is associated with the dissolution of the self, the oral person must create artificial barriers against it. His feeling about sleep has similar meaning and he both craves and fears it.

The attempts of the oral-erotic person to fill his emptiness by means of food, liquor, money, and sex bring him into conflict with the social mores, if not with the law. His constant skirmishes with people tend to intensify his expectation of rejection. He does not regard his activities as "bad" because he realizes they are necessary for his existence. He recognizes that others think they are bad, and he engages in them as part of his "testing out" of new people.

The oral-erotic person achieves his need for rejection in three ways: he re-enacts his former loss or abandonment; he incurs disapproval by his self-indulgence or acting out of his oral needs; and he expresses the rage that accumulates within him because his needs have not been met. Rage is an important characteristic of persons with oral-erotic character disorders. On the surface, they may appear easygoing and unaggressive, but a particular frustration may set off a violent explosion of anger. Their lack of control resembles the uncontrollable anger of the infant who is not fed when he is hungry; it seems to overwhelm his whole body. Their outbursts are extremely frightening to others, particularly to their children, and the persons themselves are often frightened when the attack is over. They sometimes tend to withdraw from people in order to avoid the risk of their own homicidal wrath.

One woman described an incident that took place in a bar. She said she had exploded like a volcano when a strange man made a pass at her. Although she obviously had invited his overtures, his attention somehow touched off the smoldering anger she felt toward men. Her own father had deserted her; she had had to compete with a stepfather for her mother's attention; and she had been rejected by the father of her illegitimate child. At the bar, she smashed a glass, cut the man's face with the jagged edge, threw him to the floor, and stamped on him with her spike heels. No one was able to subdue her until her mother rushed in saying, "Think of the children." Subsequently the woman became frightened by this outburst and tended to avoid people.

A "safe" form of gratification for oral-erotic women is to shower love on small babies or on animals. When their babies begin to grow up and demand more mature mothering, these women are helpless. They have no pattern for dealing with the child's later problems, and they have a strong tendency to repeat the rejection or abandonment that they experienced as children. This may also account for their frequent and ambivalently expressed wish for separation or for placement for their children.

During periods of withdrawal and diminished acting out, people with oral-erotic character disorders are likely to show a variety of physical symptoms. For instance, Mrs. Hart, who was mentioned earlier, had gastrointestinal symptoms, recurrent kidney ailments, and heart symptoms for which little physical basis could be found. Nevertheless, she had frequent acute attacks, so that during a three-year period she had last rites administered four times. On one occasion, when she was confined to bed and the district doctor and visiting nurse were in daily attendance, her husband hurt his hand at work and her favorite son was injured by an automobile. Mrs. H rose from her sickbed, cared for her husband and son, took charge of the household, and had no physical symptoms for several weeks. These people have a way of rising to an occasion, especially if it involves oral gratification. As a result, they have very rapid shifts of mood which surprise more stable people.

This variable use of physical symptoms, together with flamboyant or dramatic behavior and the tendency to sexual acting out, has resulted in confusion between persons with oral-erotic character disorders and those classified as hysterics. They are, however, much more infantile than hysterics, with less well developed egos and a need to gratify more primitive wishes. In their verbalizations as well as in their acting out there is absence of the oedipal material that characterizes the hysteric. Their sexual behavior, as we have pointed out earlier, represents a search for mothering and is not, as with the hysteric, on a heterosexual level. The dramatic quality of their behavior is also different from that of the hysteric; their drama lies in the hectic search for the euphoria of primitive gratification rather than in the complicated fantasy of oedipal gratification.[4] Life is rarely dull for the oral-erotic. If gratification is not forthcoming, he must precipitate crises to ward off his depression. He knows that he is alive only when things are happening.

An oral-erotic mother who becomes an agency client inevitably repeats her characteristic behavior with the social worker, who is regarded as a potential source of mothering, whether the worker is a woman or a man. The client immediately begins to struggle with the conflict between her wish for gratification and her expectation of rejection. Contact with the worker is perceived as dangerous as well as desirable. The client may sense that the enormity of her needs will doom her to rejection; she also senses, and has a fear of, the depression that inevitably will overcome her if she is made aware of the bottomless pit of her unmet needs. She is ashamed of the infantile part of herself. She may try to appear grown up, but she is unable to sustain this role very long. Consciously she knows that her past or present unacceptable behavior, such as drinking or promiscuity, will incur disapproval if it becomes known. Her fear of revealing herself is heightened by her awareness of her inner rage, which she perceives as homicidal. She is thus caught between her wishes for gratification and her rage and depression at the idea that her needs will never be met. Part of her rage stems from the fact that she feels so isolated from people who do not understand her needs.

Consequently, such a client will test the worker repeatedly in ways designed to provoke the expected rejection. Some of the characteristic methods of testing include breaking appointments, acting-out behavior, withdrawal, and making demands. Also, the client may offer small revelations of misbehavior as trial balloons to test the degree of acceptance. These maneuvers will be discussed further in the chapters on treatment.

---

4 Compare Lucille N. Austin, "Dynamics and Treatment of the Client with Anxiety Hysteria," *Ego Psychology and Dynamic Casework*, Howard J. Parad (ed.), Family Service Association of America, New York, 1958, pp. 137–158.

The Ball Family

The Ball case is a fairly typical example of the family and household of an oral-erotic mother. The family was referred to a child guidance clinic after the two daughters, Judy, 12, and Betty, 9, were caught stealing purses in a department store. In addition, there was one son, Donald, 11, and a stepfather who was in the merchant marine and away much of the time. Mrs. B, age 33, appeared dull at first. She had a shapeless, obese body, an expressionless face, and long hair straggling about her shoulders. She spoke without animation about the girls' stealing, wondering what she had done wrong. Had she been too easy or too strict? She thought maybe she watched over Judy too much or expected too much of her. She had relied on her a lot for the care of the younger children. She spoke of her own struggles to make ends meet. She added that, at least since her remarriage four years ago, she had had more money than before. This seemed to be self-reproach for not being able to manage better. She began to depreciate herself in other ways, ending by saying that she knew she was childish and therefore could not control her children. If she died, someone else could do better with them.

In speaking of the family's health, she told of her own headaches and menstrual difficulties. She had been told that she should have a hysterectomy but she was afraid that she would feel empty. Besides, she wanted a baby for her present husband. She berated herself for her inability to diet. "I was able to give up smoking and drinking, but not eating." She spoke of her reliance on her church and on her former mother-in-law who lived downstairs in the same house. It was brought out in the interview that seven years earlier Mrs. B had come to the city to visit her mother-in-law and had remained. When asked if Judy had been afraid of coming to the clinic, Mrs. B said she herself had been more afraid. The caseworker told her about the plan for a diagnostic study to see what kind of help Judy needed. Mrs. B's response was, "The worst thing about me is my temper. I blow up and then I hit the children."

Mrs. B did not keep her next appointment. Judy came alone and asked the psychologist whether a girl could continue to come to the clinic if her mother did not come. The caseworker wrote to Mrs. B, saying that she hoped Mrs. B would come the following week. Again Judy came alone and told the psychologist a story about a girl whose mother was afraid to go to a clinic because she used to drink and leave the children alone and she was ashamed of it. The following week, after writing to Mrs. B, the caseworker made a home visit.

The family lived on the top floor of a rickety building in a run-down neighborhood. The kitchen was sunny, cheerful, and clean, though cluttered with numerous gadgets. There were many dogs and cats which were introduced and admired. Some belonged to one member of the family and others belonged to everybody. The mother's dog was called "Baby" and Judy's was "Lady." Finally the caseworker asked if Mrs. B had found it difficult to return to the clinic. She nodded, saying, "I guess I talked out of turn. I have no right to bother other people with my troubles." In an effort to control herself, she went to the sink and filled a pan of water for one of the dogs. She talked in a jumble of words about being childish and having trouble with money. She guessed she needed a budget. She disregarded an offer of help in this direction. She did agree to try to come to the clinic the following week.

She did not come then, but she did come for a joint conference with the psychiatrist. Here she repeated much that she had already said about her own childishness and expecting too much of Judy. She had begun to wonder if there was any supervised recreational group that Judy might join.

We told Mrs. B that we recommended continued treatment for Judy and regular contact for Mrs. B. We stressed Judy's confusion about whether she wanted to be big or little and the fact that she was not working up to capacity in school. Mrs. B was somewhat aware of both problems and expressed concern about them. However, she mentioned that the other two children also had problems. She thought that Betty had really been the instigator in the shoplifting, and she feared that Donald was "like his father." She appeared to be defending Judy by telling of the deficiencies of the others. (However, it eventually became clear that she felt inadequate with all three and wanted help for them all.) She agreed to weekly appointments for herself.

After the psychiatrist had left the room, the caseworker said that, like Judy, Mrs. B seemed to want help, but that it was difficult for her to come to the clinic. She nodded and said that it was not that she did not want to come, but it was hard for her to leave the house. The worker asked if she felt worse after she had been here. She said that she felt "lighter," but only for a few days.

In the months that followed, Mrs. B talked intensely about herself, making little pretense of coming to talk about Judy. Any subject led directly to her own feelings. But she did not keep regular appointments. Judy, in her therapy during these early months, demonstrated that her own needs and wishes were secondary to those of her mother. Much of her material in interviews and tests sounded like a continuation of her mother's conversation about wanting a baby. Judy wanted to make dolls for her mother, and when she went to a store with her therapist, she wanted to buy a teddy bear for her mother. Her stealing of the purses seemed related to her mother's threatened loss of femininity through surgery.

Mrs. B could give history only in brief references to her past. This piecemeal material may be summarized as follows:

Mrs. B was born when her own mother was 14 years old. Until the age of eleven Mrs. B believed that her grandmother was her mother. Her real mother, who was in and out of the household, was married to a much older man whom she later divorced, after the birth of two more children. The grandmother placed these children for adoption. The mother died of cancer at the age of 25. It was then that Mrs. B discovered that this woman was her mother. Mrs. B was deeply attached to her and had been aware of the affection shown her by this young woman when the grandmother was not around. Mrs. B then divided her concept of mothers into the young, beautiful, and good, and the old, mean, and cruel. The grandmother punished her sadistically after the mother's death, and Mrs. B began to search for a "good mother."

Mrs. B apparently showed her grief by acting-out activities in the community and by opposing her grandmother, but the details are not clear. However, after she had received a severe beating from the grandmother, relatives intervened and the child was removed from the grandmother and placed in a home for dependent children. Mrs. B recalled that during the first year there she was "unbelievably awful" and got along with nobody. She did well in her studies and later grew to love the place. She was especially interested in dramatics, writing plays, and taking comic parts. In adolescence, she was given a work placement with a motherly "Mama Hicks" who ran a nursing home. Mrs. B recalled being happy there and enjoying caring for the old people.

When Mama Hicks became ill and gave up the home, Mrs. B was inconsolable. She failed to adjust in other work homes and was returned to the institution.

At the age of 21 she went to live with a cousin and got a job in a factory. Her cousin was having marital difficulties and because of the fighting Mrs. B became so frightened that she accepted Mr. B's offer of marriage after a short acquaintance. She seems to have been attracted chiefly to his mother. Mrs. B said she never enjoyed sexual relations, but felt she had to accede to Mr. B's demands in return for a home—which he never provided. He had fathered a baby by another woman to whom he returned after he was discharged from the army. His mother later persuaded him to return to Mrs. B and their two children, but after Mrs. B became pregnant with Betty, the mother-in-law helped her to leave her husband, since he was beating her and running around with other women.

At the time of the divorce, Mrs. B allowed her husband to keep Judy because she thought her mother-in-law would continue to care for the child. However, Mr. B remarried and he and his wife took Judy and neglected and mistreated her. When Mrs. B discovered this, she petitioned to regain custody, which was granted. Later she joined her mother-in-law in another city where she began drinking and running around, frequently neglecting the children. She married her second husband because he was insistent and because she thought he would provide for her and the children. Her second husband was a cook on a ship and was away for months at a time. Even after this marriage, she continued to drink and run around. In interviews she referred frequently to the fact that she had suddenly given up drinking after she saw what drink did to a friend of hers. This friend was a girl who had been seduced by her father and had had a baby by her brother. Mrs. B had taken care of this child and had been heartbroken when the girl took him away from her and placed him. Apparently this action followed some trouble between the two women. Mrs. B said the girl was jealous of her success with men when they went on double dates, although the men "meant nothing" to Mrs. B. Whenever Mrs. B talked of her difficulty in trusting anyone she always referred to this girl.

In the first nine months of treatment, Mrs. B was seen only nine times, which included two home visits. The recurrent themes in her interviews throw light on the broken appointments. She talked of withdrawal from people and her fear of going out. She spoke about her former drinking, stressing that it had been severe, but that she had given it up suddenly. She said that with her it was "all or nothing." She denied any problem about drinking now, but it seemed that not going out was a defense against it. She also spoke of not trusting people, saying that it was better to be alone. The only friends whom she mentioned were girls with illegitimate babies or whose husbands had deserted—people who were more unfortunate than herself. She showed some uneasiness about the children's going to camp and preferred that they go at different times, implying that they were a protection for her.

Another theme she reiterated was that she did not deserve love. She wanted to work in order to be with people but she felt that nobody wanted her. She referred to being exploited on former jobs and how this had angered her. She was afraid she might kill someone when she was angry. "I guess I have the devil in me." She recognized the contradictions in her feelings and behavior and asked if she were crazy. She expressed a fear that the children would become stupid like their father or crazy (presumably like her). She berated herself for her inability to diet, saying, "I know calories, and my house is full of diets, but I get a feeling inside that hurts and then when I take something forbidden I feel good." She expressed guilt about having left Judy with the father for a time after she and her husband separated. She spoke regretfully of her own childishness. "I can't help the children unless I help myself." She continued to wish for a baby; she and her husband had even gone for fertility tests. Although she had spoken of her earlier wish to be a boy, she told with pleasure that the doctor had said that she now had such a large supply of hormones that she was "more of a girl than ever." She had a fantasy about moving to the country, which was obviously a wish to return to her old home.

In these recurrent themes one sees the whole struggle of the oral-erotic character. Mrs. B believed that the only way to gain love was to be a baby, but she recognized that this idea was in contradiction to the ideas of the adult world. She knew that being childish would cause rejection. To her, adults were dangerous, since they rejected, exploited, blamed, betrayed, or deserted others; contact with them led her to depression, acting out, rage, and craziness. The only safe solution she could find was to give love and nurture to a baby or to return literally to childhood. Once she said that she really felt comfortable only with animals.

During these initial nine months she divulged little about her current life, except for occasional references to a gynecological difficulty for which she attended a medical clinic, and some complaints about Judy's being saucy, defiant, and careless about bathing and chores. She did mention that her first husband had come to visit his mother and had taken Donald fishing. His cousin had told her that the father had given Donald sex information "of the wrong kind." She was upset, recognizing that interference by her would be interpreted by Donald as opposition to his seeing his father.

In later months, Mrs. B revealed that the children's father was now living downstairs with his mother, having left his third wife. Mrs. B then expressed concern about his affectionate advances toward Judy, but said that she never left them alone. She made it clear that she would oppose any plan to separate Judy from her. She did allow her to join a recreational and therapeutic group organized by another agency.

An incestuous relationship between Judy and her father now came to light. The incest was multiply determined. The mother's helplessness about adolescent problems and her overprotection of the children at some points, coupled with neglect at others, unquestionably contributed to the girl's susceptibility. Also, Judy was constantly stimulated to sexual interest by her mother's openly expressed wish for a baby. Mrs. B obviously had no idea about setting limits for Judy's dating or helping her to develop any controls; when a boy asked her to go to the movies, the mother forbade it. In discussing her handling of Judy, Mrs. B said sadly that she did not know how to treat older children. It seemed to her that she had been a baby and then was suddenly expected to be grown up—with nothing in between. She had allowed Judy to go to the movies with the father whom she mistrusted, and she sometimes left her alone at home. Meanwhile Mrs. B talked constantly of babies and she bought a nesting cage for the parakeets.

When the incest was discovered, Mrs. B had to be restrained forcibly from killing her former husband. She spoke openly and unashamedly of her wish to "castrate him." At times, her perception of her own part in it would emerge and she would say, "It's my own fault. I left her as bait. It would have been better if I had given in to him myself." There was some indication that his sadism still held some erotic attraction for her.

During the next few days, on the numerous trips to police stations and courts, she was accompanied by all three children, whom she led about the city with a kind of competent generalship. While waiting on benches the younger children played "hangman." After one especially gruelling court hearing, the caseworker took Mrs. B and the children to a restaurant where they had a hilarious lunch, behaving as if this were a pleasant holiday. Once they had left the table, the mother's gloom descended upon her again and she expressed fear that Judy was pregnant or that she might repeat the incestuous act. At night when there was no activity in the house, Mrs. B became even more depressed and had thoughts of suicide, mixed with regret that she had not killed the father when she had the chance.

Her fear of the pregnancy soon turned into anticipation. She and Judy acted as if the pregnancy were an established fact and talked about keeping the baby. There was obvious disappointment when the tests proved negative. Although, at the height of the furor, Mrs. B had asked for placement of Judy in a boarding school, she was soon reluctant even to consider camp. In the fall, when the issue of placement was raised by the caseworker at the request of Judy's therapist, Mrs. B not only objected verbally but avoided the caseworker, even to the extent of being out or having the downstairs door locked when she knew a visit was to be made. She then began to find reasons for communicating with Judy's therapist who became the "beautiful young lost mother" while the caseworker seemed to be relegated to the role of the "mean old grandmother." Mrs. B was not able to resume a meaningful contact with the caseworker until many months later and not until she had had considerable reassurance that placement would not be made against her will and that the worker still accepted her. Part of the demonstration of acceptance was the initiation of treatment for the two younger children.

The Oral-sadistic Personality

Oral-sadistic parents are more likely to have contact with courts and public welfare agencies than with clinics or voluntary agencies. They rarely ask for service, but are frequently involved in court actions or in complaints about neglect of children. If they do ask for service, they tend to antagonize the caseworker or psychiatrist by their hostile and provocative behavior. They sometimes cover their hostility with an extremely thin layer of obsequiousness which often makes the other person more uncomfortable than overt hostility. They expect rejection and provoke it. The help offered is never the right thing or enough to meet their expectations.

Mr. O'Neill, who was known intermittently to a family service agency, managed to alienate a good many of the townspeople where he lived. He and his wife always seemed to call attention to their poverty in a way that made other people feel guilty about having anything. Church groups would collect clothing for them, only to find that within a matter of days the children looked as ragged and dirty as before. The church women who visited always noted the bareness and the stale smell of the home, and the apparent unwelcomeness of any offering. When a job was found for Mr. O'N as assistant janitor in a local church, the family did not cease its demands for emergency help and Mr. O'N had soon antagonized the janitor as well as the minister and the church wardens. The children, on the whole, withdrew from other children at school, but occasionally tormented some smaller child in the neighborhood. They played together at home, usually looking listless and pale. The only exception was the oldest girl who seemed to act like a mother or an older sister to the mother. She was better nourished and more self-possessed than her younger siblings and did well in school, but she seemed to repulse friendship by her rather distant and calculating attitude. Although it seemed probable that both Mr. and Mrs. O'N did some drinking, this never emerged as a problem. However, in this type of family there is often a kind of family protectiveness which succeeds in concealing such problems from outsiders.

This kind of protectiveness often colors the history which oral-sadistic clients give and, as a result, the caseworker has to make surmises about their background. The staff of a nursery school in a slum area was puzzled about aloofness of two mothers who were sisters. Finally, it was learned from an old social agency record that the women as girls had protected their alcoholic mother against numerous investigations by public welfare workers. Their extreme reticence, therefore, was not surprising.

34

The children of a mother with an oral-sadistic character disorder have difficulty in accepting the fact that she has little to give them. Much of their acting out is related to their need to cling desperately to the hope that the parents will give them affection. Carol Wing at 14 was apprehended for stealing with other girls in the neighborhood. She was placed on probation and did well until her older sister returned home with her illegitimate baby. The baby occupied the center of Mrs. W's attention. Carol, who was asthmatic, had been receiving some attention as the result of her illness. Since both the mother and grandmother were asthmatic, the asthma appeared to be a type of pathological mother-daughter tie. Mrs. W herself spoke with emotion of the asthma, indicating that it was something which she and Carol shared—almost as if it were a valuable inheritance. With the coming of the baby, Carol lost her advantageous position and, in response to the deprivation, she ran away to another city, where she promptly gave herself up to the authorities. She had no idea how to maintain herself. Later, because of her violated probation, she was placed in a girls' reformatory, where she soon became ill with asthma and had to be transferred to a hospital. Subsequently she had a number of placements. The asthma, which continued to be a problem, was multiply determined. Living closely with other girls in the reformatory recreated her competitive feelings toward her sisters and the infantile homosexual tie to her mother. Asthma (as well as holding her breath until almost choking) had been her usual outlet for tension and a source of secondary gain by evoking attention from her mother. When Carol was later placed in a small home for asthmatics, run by a motherly, understanding woman, she at first made progress. Subsequently her demands became excessive and when they were not met she turned on the foster mother with murderous rage. Upon her return to the reformatory, she repeated the behavior toward other mother figures; it was finally found necessary to place her in a mental hospital. Throughout these various placements she begged continuously to be sent home to her mother.

Mrs. W was a small, emaciated woman who, at 36, had had eleven children, five of whom had died. She suffered from a variety of illnesses, in addition to asthma. She gave the impression, alternately, of being very young or prematurely old. Mr. W was a chronic alcoholic who was usually unemployed; the family was usually dependent on public assistance. Mrs. W, who was the more verbal of the parents, was always full of complaints about the way they had been treated by welfare workers, probation officers, and so forth. She rarely had a good word to say of anyone. Once, when she complained that it was hard for her to go to see Carol, the social worker made plans to drive Mr. and Mrs. W in her car. As might be anticipated, they were not ready when the worker called for them. They complained about everything on the journey and insisted on stopping along the way to buy things.

Summary

The person with an oral character disorder presents problems to everyone. To himself, he presents the problem of depressed feelings, a haunting sense of childishness and failure, and a feeling of being an outcast. He gives inconsistent nurture to his children when they are young and is unable to help them with their later problems of development. He offers them a faulty ego ideal, since his own weak ego results in lack of impulse control and confused perception of reality.

These persons present problems to the community. They often need financial assistance and free medical care. They are in conflict with various community standards, and frequently they themselves and their children come to the attention of courts. They present special problems to the social worker who attempts to help them with any of these problems. They are difficult to engage in a relationship and when a relationship is established, considerable time and patient work are required before their patterns of behavior begin to change. Agencies are in a difficult position in dealing with their disturbed behavior, since it not only creates many real difficulties but often tends to provoke retaliation on the part of the staff who may also exhibit excessive demands, hostility, rejection, and punishment in ways which recapitulate the pathology rather than working it through. Authoritative action, which is frequently necessary, is effective only if it takes into account the meaning of the behavior and has itself the attributes of a good parental role.

III. The Anal Character Disorder

PERSONS WHOSE CHARACTER DISORDERS are rooted primarily in the anal stage of development are sometimes difficult to identify. They do not represent such definite types as do persons with oral character disorders. They manifest a wider range of personality traits and characteristics. Since the anal stage of development covers approximately the period from eighteen months to three years and includes an extensive process of training, the character formation may represent a fixation at any point in the course of this developmental stage.

During the anal stage, the developmental tasks include both the process of toilet training and learning to speak. At this stage, the child still relates to people as a source of supply for his needs, but in a different way from his earlier pattern. In the oral stage, the parent seemed to know what he needed and seemed to supply it magically; the child felt omnipotent because of his undifferentiated object relationship. In the anal stage, he still believes in magic but he perceives the magic as coming from the parent; he now invests the parent instead of himself with omnipotence. This partial differentiation of self and non-self is an advance in development. The child now must conform to the demands of the omnipotent parents in order to obtain parental love and necessary supplies. The process of learning to conform therefore engenders a picture of conditional love—if the child is dry, he is loved. Such conditional terms for receiving love inevitably lead the child toward manipulating his parents. He will give only if he receives. If he meets the conditions and does not get the expected reward, he naturally becomes angry. This situation is crucial in the development of character disorders because the child is at the height of the conflict between instinctual gratification and gratification through control, and requires the reward of love to give up the former. Under normal circumstances, with sufficient love and approval, the child will progress in the developmental process and incorporate the parental attitudes and values. In other words, the way in which the conditional love is worked out will determine whether his personality will become fixated at this point and, if it is, whether it will be at the anal-erotic or the anal-sadistic level.

The child at this stage does not yet make sexual differentiations between male and female. Men and women are classified by such criteria as activity or passivity and strength or weakness. In the persons who develop anal character disorders, such stereotyped thinking about behavior persists, becoming a source of confusion in their perception of reality. People and their actions are viewed as black or white, strong or weak, and right or wrong. In other words, the conception of maleness or femaleness is based not on a sexual identification but rather on an idea of how men or women should act. The child at the anal stage shows his unresolved identity but, whether boy or girl, the child is in the process of incorporating both masculine and feminine characteristics. Since sexual identification does not come until the oedipal conflict has been resolved, persons with character disorders have many vestiges of bisexuality. This is especially true of the anal-erotic person who is fixated at the "messy" defiant stage; he usually takes pleasure in both male and female characteristics.

The anxiety that the child feels in the anal stage is related primarily to the threat of separation from parent figures. This anxiety is often concentrated on a concern over loss of body excreta which is a precursor of castration anxiety. The difference between excreta anxiety and castration anxiety lies in the child's preoccupation in the former with possessions or accomplishments as a means of gaining security rather than in his fear of bodily harm. Bowel movements, money, or sex pleasure come to stand for love. Castration anxiety does not evolve until the child has made sufficient object differentiation to focus his libidinal energy on the concept of sexuality as a meaningful relationship between two people. This process is part of the resolution of the oedipal conflict. During the anal phase, in contrast, the urgent problems of bowel and bladder control are central, and the pattern established becomes the prototype for control over emotions and the dangers of affective explosions. Since control over excreta is such an important issue in the conditional love offered by parents at this stage, the loss of control is particularly threatening.

Typical Features

Personality features associated with the anal stage of development occur in a variety of psychological disturbances including not only character disorders but obsessive compulsive neuroses and psychoses. The personality differences are based on the ego's development and its organization of the instinctual forces associated with the anal stage. Persons with character disorders who are fixated at the anal level of development show a much more poorly organized ego structure with more inconsistent behavior and less conformity to community norms than do the compulsive neurotics.

Persons suffering from anal character disorders are characterized by ambivalence, omnipotence, and bisexuality. These persons tend to think in opposites, sharply dividing love and hate, strength and weakness, goodness and badness, and sanity and "craziness." Such stereotyped thinking naturally affects the parent's handling of his child, both in the early training and later in reaction to the child's antisocial behavior. This tendency to deal in opposites is, of course, inherent in the parent's perception of his own behavior. A woman, for instance, will believe that if she ever slips from her strict standard of morality she will become a prostitute. It is not uncommon to find an adolescent daughter and her mother each trying to use a psychiatrist as an ally in their battle to settle which one is sane and which is crazy. If one is one way, the other must be the opposite.

Mothers and fathers in this group constantly use the giving and withholding of favors as a way of training their children. When they give, they expect gratitude or repayment and are bitterly disappointed if neither is forthcoming. A common complaint of such a parent is, "I took Johnnie to the circus and he was just as bad the next day." The parent is preoccupied with fairness, equality, truth, and justice. He is often literal to an extreme and denies the existence of feelings—both his own and the feelings of others. In his struggle for his rights, justice, or vindication, he often tries to force the caseworker to take one side or the other. He believes that one must be either for him or against him. Such ambivalence is different from the ambivalence of the oral character whose concept of "for or against" is in terms of "what is good is inside and what is bad is outside."

In the person with anal characteristics, the need for omnipotence is expressed in the feeling that he is safe only so long as he is in control. Essentially, it is his own impulses that he fears, whether he sees evidence of them in others or in himself. He is constantly looking for an omnipotent figure to protect him. Often his request for help with his problem child is made at a time when his magical devices to control his environment seem to be failing. He asks that someone stronger take over. He has such severe anxiety about "not knowing" that he constantly invades the child's privacy by reading his mail and asking the therapist what the child is talking about. As is true of oral characters, these parents have not made an adequate separation from the child. However, the fusion is of a different quality. It is not a matter of the same corporate identity, but the parent has a need to continue control of the child's impulses. The parent often has a feeling that he knows what his child is going to do or what he has just done. This feeling frightens him, especially if the child does not conform to his demands. He usually fails to help his children develop controls of their own, believing that only the parent can control effectively. His fear that his child is "getting away with something" expresses his inner conviction that impulses (including his own) are always bad and in danger of breaking loose.

Many people with anal character disorders place great reliance on intellectual control; they isolate thought from feeling and deny feeling. Denial and avoidance are common defenses. These people tend to emphasize "secrets," which represent some phase of their own forbidden pregenital impulses including incest fantasies, bisexual fantasies, and masturbation guilt. A person, for instance,

40

may have difficulty in discussing the parentage of his adopted child or in talking about the sexual interests or activities of his children. He relates these events to pregenital impulses rather than to adult ideas of sexuality. In one family, the father's imprisonment was treated as a guilty secret and never mentioned to his child, although the latter was four years old at the beginning of the imprisonment and had confused and troubling memories of that period. Such a secret can have a strangely disturbing effect on family relationships; it exists as a kind of no man's land which becomes highly important because of the unspoken taboos surrounding it. The problems associated with secrets as they relate to treatment will be discussed in later chapters.

One of the most important defense mechanisms of the person with an anal character disorder is activity. This is also true of the obsessive, compulsive neurotic, but its expression takes somewhat different forms. The activity of a person with a character disorder is likely to be less well organized, to be directed toward less sublimated ends, and to be generally less effective. Many of these people, however, are good workers until old familial stresses are recreated on the job, interfering with their relationships. Some tend to use work in an extreme way, driving themselves to the point of exhaustion. When such a person is forced by physical illness to take a rest, a severe depression is likely to ensue. These are the people who explain that they would rather work than "think."

One often finds such parents stimulating the use of defensive activity in their children. One mother, who was being interviewed in the park because she had brought along a fretful 3-year-old child, urged him constantly to "chase the pigeons." (One of the problems of her older child was hyperactivity.) Another form of activity parents use is flight. When tensions in the family become too great, many of these people have a strong impulse to "walk out." Frequently, they leave the house and walk around the block or walk for longer periods with no object in mind, returning when the tension lessens. The motive of flight is different from that of the oral person who, when he walks out, walks toward some form of gratification rather than away from tension.

In the families of parents with anal character disorders, pressure is placed on the children to meet their parents' needs, but the needs are not the same as in parents with oral character disorders. The mother, in the former instance, tends to place her daughter in the role of a sister with whom she shares her problems, and who is supposed to be her assistant in caring for the younger children and doing the housework. The mother has little or no recognition that her expectations are excessive and that the girl's emotional investment is elsewhere. As a result, major conflicts can develop between mother and daughter. A common sequence of complaints from the mother goes something like this: "Jane would rather work for the neighbors than for me . . . I can't depend on her . . . She never sees anything to do in the house . . . She leaves dirty dishes in the sink . . . And her own room is a mess." A real blow-up then takes place over the issue of the daughter's untidy bedroom. The mother's mounting anger over the girl's failure to cater to the mother's needs and feelings drives her to her only sure identification with her own anal mother—the defense of keeping things neat. Symbolically, it is the mother's way of saying to the girl, "You are a mess." Needless to say, the girl reacts and replies in like terms.

This kind of interaction stems from the fact that people with anal character disorders have a strong need for dependency gratification, which they are unable to express in any direct way because of their fear of weakness and helplessness. Since the mothers have an inadequate pattern for mothering, and get insufficient gratification from the tasks involved, they have a tendency to feel exploited and to expect someone (usually the daughter) to share the burden with them. Many of these mothers are of the "assistant mother" type, described by Helene Deutsch,[1] who can function in a maternal role only if there is a real mother in charge. They tend to try to create the same pattern with their daughters; when they meet with rebellion they feel even more exploited, helpless, and angry.

The parent with an anal character disorder is alarmed by signs of the child's growing up, especially when these signs suggest that the child is attempting to establish his sexual identity. The parent becomes anxious because his own bisexuality is threatened. The battleground between them is often smoking, use of lipstick, wearing high heels, and so forth. These symbols of sexuality usually pro-

[1] Helene Deutsch, M.D., *The Psychology of Women*, Grune and Stratton, New York, 1945, Vol. II, p. 73.

voke the parent to institute repressive measures which result only in further defiance by the child. The quarrels at this stage sometimes represent the parent's need to participate in the sex life of the child by fighting it. One finds in many of these parents an extreme preoccupation with the dating intrigues of their adolescent children. Such vicarious participation, which may include the parent of the opposite sex, explains in part the failure of these parents to impose reasonable dating limits.

The Anal-erotic Personality

Persons with anal-erotic character disorders take pleasure in "messy" and defiant behavior. Some kinship exists between them and oral-erotic persons in that both expect pleasure and have a tendency to seek direct gratifications. Anal-erotic persons, however, will not pay the price of being controlled. The fact that they can rebel against control and authority suggests that, in the oral stage of development, they received enough gratification to have an optimistic or omnipotent view of their own powers. It seems likely that they received some overstimulation which led to showing off—for example, the child taking pride in his bowel movement. They may also have shown a precocious assertion of independence. They do not repress their feelings, although they may sometimes restrain the expression of them out of fear of being controlled.

These persons show a good deal of curiosity, which is related primarily to the early phase of the anal period. They want to know so that they can control. They also have special pleasure in finding out about things that are forbidden or hidden. Their use of activity is more imaginative and creative than that of the anal-sadistic person. They often have a flair for artistic pursuits, especially if these involve using ingenuity. They will go out of their way to invent and improvise, rather than follow directions or imposed patterns. They enjoy doing things "differently" and usually do poorly on routine or repetitive jobs.

The bisexuality of these persons is very clear. They want the attributes which they associate with both male and female and offer resistance to giving up either one during the treatment process. A mother may identify strongly with her son's "little boy" maleness, but will alternately fear and enjoy vicariously the signs of his

43

developing adult maleness. She may identify with the latency bi-sexuality of her daughter, but is likely to discourage adolescent femininity which represents weakness and vulnerability to her. The father is threatened by the development of maleness in his son, but tries to emphasize the maleness of his daughter. Both parents are likely to act as if they were older siblings to their children, since they find it difficult to assume a real parental role.

Since rebellion against authority is such a motivating force in these parents, they offer the child a pattern that can easily lead to his acting out the parents' conflicts, whether these are expressed in overt behavior or only in general attitudes. The child has difficulty in developing an ego ideal that is consistent with the demands of the community. Because these parents are unable to give up their own delinquent behavior or rebellious attitudes, they are often resistant to casework help. Also, their fear of a close relationship—which carries with it the danger of being controlled or of possible homosexual involvement—creates obstacles to treatment. At the same time, their strong wish for dependency, alternating with an avowed aim to be completely independent, causes marked incon-sistency in behavior. The two-sidedness of their feelings toward using help should be borne in mind in working with these people.

The marriages of anal-erotic people are apt to be unstable because of the competition for both the male and female roles, and the wish to be alternately child and parent. The result may be a separation or an uneasy balance with both partners taking both male and female roles.

The following referral statement from an authoritative agency contains a good description of a mother with an anal-erotic char-acter disorder:

> Our complaint was concerned with Mrs. Groom's leaving her children alone for days at a time, and sending them to school poorly dressed and malodorous. Because of poor attendance the children did poorly in their school work. Despite efforts to have her come to discuss these problems, the mother refused to do so and generally showed hostility toward the Sister in charge of the parochial school and toward the local priest.
>
> Mrs. G is a large, heavy-set woman, quite attractive in ap-pearance. She obviously was trying hard to impress me as being shrewd and intelligent. Her manner was one of hostile de-

fensiveness. She denied that she neglected the children and cried in a dramatic fashion. She said, "A woman is entitled to a good cry, isn't she?" She tried in many ways to put me off. She said, "I'm too upset to talk about this. I want you to do me a favor. Don't come back for two weeks. By that time I'll be able to talk to you."

Mrs. G referred vaguely to her own childhood as an unhappy one, saying she was raised by an aunt. She spoke of her inability to trust anyone—particularly the worker—and of her dedication to the children for whom she had worked so hard. Her husband had deserted about eight years before. After a period of receiving public assistance, Mrs. G had worked as a waitress. Jean, the oldest daughter, appeared to be the one who had to look after the children while her mother worked.

After a few difficult and painful interviews with Mrs. G, I went on vacation for a month. Upon returning I tried to see her, but was unsuccessful. I went to the diner where she worked but was unable to get her to discuss an appointment with me. Finally, I managed to find her at home and learned that her son James had been taken to court following his attempt to commit an unnatural act on a 10-year-old boy. His mother expressed a willingness to co-operate with the recommendations of the court clinic, but she did not have any real insight into James's problem. Her attitude was that the boy made a mistake and everyone is entitled to make a mistake once. Furthermore, she attributed James's behavior to the fact that two years before he himself had had an unnatural act committed upon him by some older boys in the same neighborhood.

Three months passed before Mrs. G and James were seen at the clinic. She failed to keep the first appointment we gave her and was finally summoned to court again for failing to carry out any of its recommendations, which included giving up her job. The court requested that the clinic wait until she complied with court recommendations before making another appointment. The following is an excerpt from the first interview at the clinic:

Mrs. G is a tall woman, stout through the middle but with slim wrists and ankles. Her hair was pulled back tight and she wore dangling earrings with red stones. She said that she and James had got lost and she was not used to walking so far in high heels. "How often do I have to come? Frankly, I don't like it." She complained that she had been taken to court because she had not responded to a letter from the clinic. She said the letter probably never was sent. I said quietly that I had mailed it myself. She then talked about the unreliability of the mails. She expressed anger about being forced to give up her job. The children had been alone only about an hour each morning and evening; they are good kids and she was not worried about them. She was just about to get a raise, too. She complained about her treatment by public assistance workers, and of her difficulty in getting medical care. Her worker, Miss F, was very strict and unsympathetic. Mrs. G mimicked her, rapping on the table and ordering Mrs. G to come back to the room when she went out to get a cleaning tissue.

Mrs. G expressed anger at the probation officer for sending her to the clinic. She thought the whole situation had been exaggerated. James was very good now and she did not expect any more trouble. She said that all children do some bad things. She remembered doing forbidden things like climbing on cliffs and going into vacant houses. I agreed that as children we all had done forbidden things and added that all children had curiosity about sex. Mrs. G said bitterly that James was forgetting all about the experience and now it was all being opened up again. I said it was too bad if a child was made to feel that he was bad or that sex was bad and dirty. Mrs. G seemed relieved about this. I explained that the purpose of the study at the clinic was to decide whether or not James should have continuing treatment. Mrs. G wanted to know if the doctor would make him talk about his sexual experience. I said the doctor wouldn't force him to talk about anything he didn't want to talk about. Again Mrs. G seemed relieved.

Mrs. G asked if she could smoke. She always smoked when she was tense and the last couple of days she had been smoking a great deal. The previous night she could not sleep. I asked her if it was because of her fear of coming to the office and she nodded. She spoke of having the ADC worker call her down for smoking while she was interviewing her. Then she said, "You people seem OK—not like them. You seem human." She added that she liked the new probation officer and that she had had ADC workers whom she liked.

In talking about James, Mrs. G admitted that he and Bobby (two years younger) truanted from school a year ago, but not since they changed schools two months ago. She told something of James's health history, speaking with real sympathy of the time he was in the hospital at Christmas with scarlet fever. She spoke with pride of how well her children were getting along together. When they watched TV they sat two on one chair.

Mrs. G made several references to "when I broke up my marriage" twelve years ago. She had not seen Mr. G for nine years and did not know where he now was. He was a wonderful guy

46

when he was sober. She had married him against her parents' wishes. She made several references to her mother, saying she was very strict. Mrs. G was the youngest of four and the only girl. She said her mother was really her aunt, since her own mother died when she was an infant. The aunt took all four children, but Mrs. G was the only one who was actually adopted. She said her children could never get away with anything because she "knew all the tricks." She knew what they were going to do even before they did it. She told how, as a child, she used to tease her brothers. If one of them came from school and took the last piece of cake, she would screech, "Ma, he's eating my cake," even though she had already had her piece. Her mother would make the brother give it to her. Apparently she is now on good terms with her brothers and they do many things for her.

I encouraged Mrs. G to talk more about having been forced to give up her work. She complained about the trouble in getting reimbursed from ADC for medical bills, but this did not seem to be the real issue. I suggested that possibly she felt she was being controlled by the welfare department. She said it was not that, but she liked to feel that the money she had was her own—not charity. She then burst into tears and shook all over. She regained her composure quickly but could not explain her feeling. I asked if she felt better when she worked. She said warmly that she did—that her life had more purpose. She gave a rapid account of what her week had been like when she worked, but made no mention of housework. She spoke of feeling at peace on Sunday, sitting and watching TV. She admitted that she felt depressed when she was at home all the time.

We talked further about plans for the study. I said I hoped she would not feel so afraid about coming next time and she said laughingly that she would not.

In these short excerpts, we get not only a picture of the main traits of the anal-erotic person, but a glimpse of the typical resistances to treatment. These will be discussed further in the section on treatment.

The Anal Sado-masochistic Personality

The person with a sado-masochistic character disorder is on the other end of the anal scale from the anal-erotic person. The latter is fixated at an early phase of development and as a result is more volatile in feeling than the anal sado-masochistic person. In some respects, anal sado-masochistic persons are like the oral-sadistic group; both received early nurture mixed with sadism or disregard of feelings. Both also developed partial identification with a controlling and denying mother. Persons with anal sado-masochistic character disorders can experience closeness best through fighting, since this has been their major experience in close relationships. They are more comfortable in expressing hostility than tenderness. Affection, however, can be tolerated during a "making-up" phase after an explosion of violence. The violence itself does not evoke so much guilt as it does in neurotics but, rather, brings a sense of relief because of the discharge of tension.

Social workers tend to expect that persons will feel guilty after an expression of overt aggression. They sometimes are surprised to find that a husband or wife feels less depressed and able to function better after a physical fight in which they threw things at each other. An adolescent girl in an institution stated that the staff members were always insisting that she must feel guilty after she had "blown up" and hit another girl, whereas the truth was that she felt a kind of calm and a sense of relief. She said she knew that she must try to get over these outbursts because they made everybody angry with her, but that they certainly made her feel good.

Many people with anal-sadistic character disorders have some inhibition against expressing anger physically, but they give verbal expression to it continually. One woman client, Mrs. Russo, after she felt comfortable with the caseworker, described with great enjoyment the verbal battles and sadistic teasing that went on between her and her adolescent son, John. She finally admitted that she preferred him to his more conforming sister because he had "such cute ways." Such verbal hostility is usually combined with an almost complete unawareness of the other person's feelings. This same mother told an incident about the death of her son's beloved parakeet. The daughter came into the room, saying, "Dicky is asleep on the bottom of the cage." Mrs. R said, "No, he's dead." She shouted upstairs, "Johnny, Dicky is dead." John came downstairs and took the bird up to his room. His mother kept calling to find out what he was doing until her husband made her stop.

One important weapon of these persons in their struggle to control is "knowing." They will go to extreme lengths to find out what their children are doing or thinking. They completely disregard the normal rights of privacy that are so jealously guarded by the adolescent. These parents frequently precipitate acting-out behavior on the part of their adolescent children by searching their bureau drawers or purses, reading their mail, or resorting to trickery to learn what they have been doing. Mrs. R, for example, told several lies to her son's friend in order to trap him into telling her John smoked. In the same interview in which she told of her trickery, she complained that John lied to her.

These parents often use intellectual devices as a magical means of controlling others. They argue endlessly about rights and logic and theories, with complete disregard for the emotions and feelings of the persons involved. They constantly ask how one "is supposed" to make something come about, as if there were some rules that would make things go the way they want. Many of them believe that any situation can be altered if they make a slight change in their methods of manipulation. Their wish to manipulate creates problems for the caseworker in the early stages of treatment, and, unless he is wary, he may get drawn into environmental manipulations which have magical meanings for these clients.

When such people feel out of control, they are likely to threaten to break off a relationship with some person with the ultimatum: "This is the end." They do not literally mean the end, but the ultimatum is a signal that they have reached an end-point to the buildup of tension and that they need a "showdown" in order to relieve the strain. They then start over again with the relationship in the classically anal way. The source of their need to control is the old training struggle when the child responded to the conditional giving of love by his parents with attempts to manipulate them. The adult retains the grandiose conception, characteristic of the anal phase of psychosexual development, that he can control the actions of others. His rage stems from his feeling that he is not being given the reward he deserves—by parents, mate, child, or society—when he has symbolically produced the gift of a bowel movement.

Usually life histories given initially by parents with anal-sadistic character disorders reveal, by omissions, important sources of their deprivation. They often omit material about siblings. References to parents and childhood experiences are vague and tend to create a rosy picture of harmony between parents and children. It is only after considerable contact that one learns of the person's struggle to secure and keep a place for himself in the family and to compete successfully with other siblings for the small store of parental love that was available. Frequently he married early in an attempt to get love from a source outside the family, but he continued to try to extract something from his parents. His competition with his siblings and with their children generally remains active.

Some persons with anal character disorders have a primarily masochistic orientation, rather than a sado-masochistic one. In them, the overt expression of aggression has been strongly inhibited, and their chief motivation is hope of gratification through being good and through suffering. We have observed this orientation most often in women. Since this manifestation is diagnostically somewhat puzzling, it deserves some explanation.

Unlike psychoneurotic persons fixated at the anal sado-masochistic level, persons with character disorders do not find suffering pleasurable. These people endure or seek it with the expectation of receiving a reward.[2] A woman, for example, will show a kind of compliance with her own mother's standards of behavior but it is not wholehearted; the lack of wholeheartedness may not be evident at first. As a child, she submitted to her mother's demands because of her strong dependency needs and her fear of losing her chance of securing love from the mother. Her lack of acceptance of her mother's standards is shown only in her distorted, exaggerated form of compliance. Her lack of identification with her mother makes trouble for her in dealing with her own children. She is caught between her mother's standards and her own rebellious feelings; the latter give her some identification with her children, although she tries to suppress these feelings. Since she does not "feel like the mother," she cannot be firm with her children. She may put on a show of punishing them and disapproving of their behavior, but they are not convinced by her act. She cannot transmit standards to her children or communicate with them on a feeling level. When she tries to differentiate among her children, she becomes uncomfortable because such differentiation stirs up her own feelings

[2] Theodor Reik, *Masochism in Modern Man,* Farrar and Rinehart, New York, 1941, p. 374.

of rivalry which she tries to deny. She lives in fear of what other people will think of her, since she attributes the attitudes of her disapproving mother to the community, the school, and the neighbors. She sees her mother everywhere in fantasy. For this reason, she cannot accept reassurances that she is not "bad" or that people are not all against her; such reassurances tend to make her only more anxious. She often describes her punishment of one of her children as more sadistic than it really was in order to justify herself to her mother. One woman told with considerable feeling about punishing her child for his refusal to wash himself; the degree of her feeling suggested that it was her standards that were violated rather than the secondhand ones passed on by her mother, to which she did not fully subscribe. The two crimes forbidden by her mother had been open expression of aggression and sexuality. It was evident that the client had not given up her internalized conflict about either.

The social history of such a woman often contains a revealing statement that "her only act of rebellion was her marriage." The marriage was often an early one to someone who, for some reason, was unacceptable to her family; he also served the function of enabling her to act out her forbidden wishes or of giving gratification to her after punishment, in the way her mother had done. A further basis for the attraction probably was that the husband also was the deprived one in his family.

These masochistic women appear asexual rather than bisexual. Unlike the neurotic women who repress sexual impulses, these women retain the fantasied gratifications of the anal period. They have an everpresent need to stimulate the acting out of sexual impulses by others in order to obtain vicarious gratification. They cannot recall any true adolescent period of their own, since their relationships with boys during chronological adolescence were accompanied by severe denial and repression of their own feelings. These women often tell almost unbelievable stories of having no knowledge before marriage of sex or the reproduction process. As a result, they have great difficulty in handling the adolescent problems of their own children. They tend to encourage sexual acting out in their children by their anxious prohibitions and the "phony" character of their restrictions. Earlier, they had similar difficulties

51

in regard to their children's aggression. When these women are angry, they often fleetingly express a wish to be "bad" sexually; they are likely to speak of people who have been immoral or aggressive in envious terms, saying such people have had better luck than they have had. They have the anal concept that people are either good or bad and that there is no middle-ground. When they are angry they have a tendency to accidents and self-injury. They allow themselves to be exploited through their inability to say no to the demands of others, since they are always hoping to earn love without taking the responsibility for giving it.

The real crisis for the person with a masochistic character disorder comes when his hope for eventual love and gratification is exploded. His equilibrium becomes disturbed. With the promise of love removed, the reason for enduring punishment is gone. The inevitable result is anger and depression, which may be expressed in a variety of ways—in homicidal aggression, in suicidal tendencies, or in realistic steps to improve his situation.

The following is an illustrative description of a mother with an anal character disorder with a primarily masochistic orientation. Mrs. Kane had six children, four of whom had already shown delinquent tendencies. The oldest girl, Janet, had been referred to a child guidance clinic by her mother because of running away and stealing. The second girl (the fourth child) had also been treated for a severe learning problem. Janet at this time was under the care of a youth service agency for persistent running away. The clinic's case summary, based on three years of treatment, is presented in part.

> The marital situation appears to defy any solution. We know little about Mr. K except what his wife had told us. The one time the worker saw Mr. K he lived up to her description of his behavior on similar occasions—he was charming, could not say enough about the mother's abilities, told of his efforts and plans to change the troubled situation, and could hardly be persuaded to admit any discouragement or irritation. He went out of his way to tell something that was untrue—that he had paid off the debt on his car. He did not return for future appointments.
>
> The disagreements are chronic and repetitive. Mr. K insists on continuing his self-employment as a painter. His two best seasons are autumn and before Easter. After Christmas and during the summer he earns very little. At these times he gambles desperately, hoping to "make a killing." When he gives Mrs. K too

little money for food and fails to pay the bills she puts pressure on him to get a job. He handles this by avoidance, making vague promises that he does not carry out. Another source of trouble appears to be his depressed behavior at any season of the year when the children require clothing or gifts. He accuses his wife of making too much of Christmas, saying that no one gave him anything as a child. At Christmas another source of trouble is the employees' party at the restaurant where Mrs. K works part time. Mr. K refuses to go and forbids her going, accusing her fellow employees of being immoral. He bases his accusation on the stories she has told him. Periodically he forbids Mrs. K to smoke. She has taken an increasingly rebellious attitude toward his orders of this type. She gets very angry about his lying to his customers and creditors, and about his expecting her and the children to tell such people that he is not at home.

Early in the contact, Mrs. K described her husband as selfish and domineering, saying that he ordered her around, belittled her, and was insanely jealous. At that time she described herself as being too tired to rebel. She just cried or retaliated by not answering the telephone for him, since he was not talking to her. They both used silence against each other for weeks or months at a time. It is apparent that Mrs. K has a lifelong pattern of submission and that Mr. K has replaced her own mother as the person who treated her sadistically but from whom she hoped for gratification.

At present, Mr. K often fails to get up to take his wife to work, forcing her to spend large amounts for taxi fare. He puts her out of the bed and refuses sex relations. Sometimes he wakes her by playing the radio loudly in the room where she is sleeping. Recently, he has been telling the children that their mother is drinking and going out with men on the nights when she works.

It is obvious that each parent alternates between being a controlling, punishing parent and a helpless child. To understand Mrs. K's masochistic endurance one must look at her history. She was the sixth of seven girls, and the second born to her mother's second marriage. At her birth, her mother was still depressed over the death of the next older daughter. Mrs. K was named for the doll of her dead sister, so presumably was not regarded as a very real substitute for the deceased child. The youngest sister, Helen, born only sixteen months later, was treated as "the baby" by the whole family. As Mrs. K gradually recalled childhood episodes, she told of her anger against her mother for favoring Helen. Helen got new clothes while she got hand-me-downs, and Helen did no housework while she scrubbed and cleaned in the vain hope of getting some praise or love.

Mrs. K's father was described as a silent, aloof man who came from the hill country in the Southwest. He drank a lot and ate what was set before him. He beat his wife and often the police were called. Mrs. K recalled feeling humiliated in the neighborhood. Her father showed little interest in the children and sometimes said he doubted that they were his. Mrs. K denied any feeling for him, but she remembered his hands which were often cut by the machine on which he worked. She expressed resentment because his employer laid him off when he got old. Although her mother had always belittled him and his family, after his death she married his brother.

Mrs. K reported that her mother would not allow the children to fight. In parochial school, Mrs. K was afraid of the Sisters because they were strict like her mother. Her warmest feeling about her mother concerned food, since the mother was a wonderful cook and never begrudged them anything to eat. Now when her husband complained about the children eating too much, Mrs. K was furious. She seemed also to be identified with her mother with respect to cleanliness, neatness, truthfulness, and honesty. She once said of herself, "The Yankee in me is strong and responsible—the hillbilly is irresponsible."

In Mrs. K we see the anal dichotomy, with a cleavage between the strong and weak roles, both of which she has incorporated. With the resolution of the oedipal conflict, a person does not struggle in this way with two identities, but has a cohesive self-concept in which the strong and weak are fused. The problem that is uppermost for Mrs. K is her early struggle with her mother and its repetition in her everyday life.

As is often true in such cases, Mrs. K's only act of defiance against her mother was in marrying Mr. K. She repeated her defiance later in returning to him after a separation. She stated that her attraction to him in the first place was that she had had seven dates with him before he kissed her. Although she began going with boys when quite young, and she liked to be hugged, she would not go out with one again if he tried to go further. Another reason she was attracted to Mr. K was the fact that he was the deprived one in his family. (Subsequently he has denied this.) Apparently each of them vented the fury about his own deprivation on the other person's mother, but remained only half aware of the hostile feelings toward his, or her, own.

Mrs. K's mother showed her disapproval of sexual matters by not giving her daughter any sex information, and by not speaking to her after her marriage (ostensibly because Mr. K was Protestant). Mrs. K had acute nausea during her whole pregnancy with Janet and was in labor for three days. She recalled that her mother had said that "labor pains were the worst pains in the world." Since hers were not "the worst in the world," she kept waiting for them to increase. Finally, on the third day, delivery was performed by instruments.

Janet had severe feeding problems from the start and had to be readmitted to the hospital. She was always overactive and Mrs. K spoke of her as having been "born with chorea." Once she said that she herself had been overactive until the birth of Janet. It was as if she had somehow transferred this activity to the baby.

After the birth of the third child, Mrs. K made a complaint to the draft board about her husband's gambling and lack of support. She left him and, with the three children, moved to her mother's house. She was depleted mentally and physically. Her mother fed her, bought her clothes, fixed her hair, and sent her out to get a job. Before Mr. K's induction into the army he met her on the street and said that she now looked "like the girl he had married." They had a reconciliation and she became pregnant again. Her mother was furious with her and would scarcely speak to her.

Her mother relented, however, after the birth of the baby, who had a deformity. It seems evident that the purpose of Mrs. K's self-neglect and submission to her mother was to gain her love and care.

Although Mrs. K had defied her mother only in the matter of her marriage, there is strong evidence that she never really accepted her mother's standards. For this reason, she always felt subject to punishment. Her mother made her feel guilty about aggression and sex, but she renounced neither one. In the marriage, Mr. K became the surrogate of her punishing mother as well as a vehicle for acting out her own hostility. For instance, at the beginning

55

of her clinic contact, Mrs. K quoted her husband to express her own anger and resistance, telling of his hostility against agencies and his insistence on punitive treatment of Janet. Under the influence of the caseworker's acceptance, she began to show her softer side, but in the next interview she again quoted the hostile remarks of her husband. At times she was caught between the influences of her husband and mother. On one occasion, when she was tormented by a psychotic neighbor, Mr. K urged her to "beat up" the woman, while her mother told her to "be the lady I brought you up to be." Mrs. K herself was afraid she might kill the woman; her solution was the usual flight into activity—she took a job.

Mrs. K's dilemma about punishing Janet was similar. She was pleased when her husband punished Janet, especially for not helping her, but at the same time she was identified with Janet and upset by the punishment. Since she had no standards of her own, she expected to be punished or criticized for not living up to those of her mother and to be blamed for anything that happened. She said she believed that she was "supposed to be" more punitive with Janet, and that Janet's acting out was the result of Mrs. K's being "easy with her." Her conception that more punitive methods were required of her was apparent in her report of punishing Janet by practically holding Janet a prisoner in her room, but then—to soften the picture—admitting that she let Janet have a record player and allowed her to go out some of the time. Her punishment of Janet was less severe when it was provoked by outside criticism than when she herself was angry with Janet. Among the things that made her angry with Janet were the girl's failure to keep herself clean, to wear pads during her menstrual period, and her tendency to evade responsibility for the younger children, to be defiant or uncommunicative with her mother, and to "get independent."

On the one hand, Mrs. K used Janet as a kind of sister and helper and, on the other, when Janet did something that others regarded as wrong, Mrs. K felt that she must prove that she did not condone it. The failure of her disciplinary efforts was due to the lack of conviction they carried, as well as their general inconsistency. It was demonstrated clearly that Mrs. K had never worked out her own feelings about sex and aggression and, therefore, had no standards of her own.

56

In an early interview, the caseworker suggested that the clinic contact could help Mrs. K to know what she thought about things. Almost at once, she began to talk about her anger against her mother. She said she was tired of being a "puppet" for her mother and her husband. She continued to hope, however, that her endurance and submission would pay off. For a time it seemed to do so; after Mr. K hit her for smoking on New Year's Eve he walked out, but came back very contrite.

During the first year of treatment, Mrs. K talked about leaving her husband and returning, with the children, to her mother. She learned, however, that her mother would not have her. She then consulted a lawyer who wrote a letter to her husband, which brought about some temporary improvement in his behavior. Her tendency to use outside authorities to carry out her aggression, not only against Mr. K but in other situations as well, continued for many months. She brought a court action against a man who had made sexual advances to one of the younger children in the park. Ostensibly she did so to protect other children from this experience, but she was bitterly disappointed when he was not sent to jail but was referred for psychiatric observation. Wanting the man punished was an expression of her sadism. She also tended to displace her forbidden impulses onto the children by inciting them to misbehavior. She would then want to have them punished, thereby getting displaced erotic satisfaction as well as sadistic pleasure.

Mrs. K was fearful of her own aggression. Her defenses against it were activity, flight, and self-injury. The following is a typical sequence. On a night when she and her husband were to decide whether or not he was to look for a steady job, he returned late for dinner. After Mrs. K made a sarcastic comment, Mr. K disregarded the dinner she had kept for him and cooked one for himself. For once, Mrs. K refrained from apologizing and went to her job seething with anger. After the peak of pressure in the restaurant kitchen was over, she cut her finger severely but worked several hours more, resenting the fact that no one made her stop. She got flour in the wound, which caused an infection, and then her husband was kind to her for a few days. Mrs. K told Janet (who was in a foster home) about the injury, to test her reaction, and then felt guilty because Janet seemed so upset. When she came to the clinic, her opening remark to the caseworker was, "I cut my finger to the bone."

There are many variations on the theme of masochism. Caseworkers have all had experience with the client who provokes her husband into being sadistic to her so that she can defeat him; by suffering she becomes the noble one and he, the beast. Another kind of masochistic behavior is more directly sexualized, with beating and intercourse following in rapid succession; the distortions of aggressive anxiety and sexuality are acted out in the sexual process. There is also the person who is so fearful of his own aggression that he puts himself in a position where he is controlled and then complains about it. Still another masochistic individual may devalue and defeat himself in order to be in the position of the helpless child. Sometimes these masochistic activities are carried on in such subtle ways that it is hard to detect the process and to interfere with the client's sense of having a luckless fate.

If it is clear to the caseworker, in dealing with persons with anal-masochistic character disorders, that their behavior springs from the wish for dependency which is denied, and from some form of the anal expectation of reward for suffering, his role becomes less confusing. What is required for the client's progression is a long period of treatment in which he is able to accept some degree of dependency and to begin to take some positive steps as an adult, without being overwhelmed by the feeling that unless he is helpless he will receive nothing.

Summary

In dealing with the whole gamut of behavior manifestations found in persons with anal character disorders, the caseworker must keep in mind the characteristics of the anal stage of infancy. If he does, he can more readily recognize the manifestations and treat them more effectively within the limits of the defenses. In their relationships with any substitute parental figures, these persons present special problems which include denial of dependent needs, mechanisms for control, and acting out of ambivalence—all requiring considerable adaptation of the casework method.

IV. The Phallic-urethral Level of Development

PARENTS WHO ARE PRIMARILY FIXATED at the phallic-urethral level of development seem to appear with much less frequency in the caseloads of agencies dealing with juvenile delinquents than do those with other types of character disorders. We found none in our caseload, although a few parents of a mixed type showed some phallic-urethral characteristics. A description of this stage of development may suggest some of the reasons for the failure of this group to use community services.

The phallic-urethral stage of psychosexual development is characterized by coalescence of libidinal energy which now loses its earlier diffuseness and becomes centered on the genital area. For both the boy and the girl, the overt expression of this phase is masturbation of an erectile organ. The frequent touching of the genitals by the 3- to 6-year-old child is one aspect of this process. Also, the child makes clearer differentiations between male and female identities. However, not until the resolution of the oedipal conflict does the child give up his bisexual identifications. The focusing of libidinal energy on the genital area gives rise to castration anxiety, which becomes a significant factor in the resolution of oedipal conflict.

Expressions of Conflict

It is not pertinent to this discussion to describe in detail the oedipal conflict and its resolution. However, we shall review cer-

59

tain concepts that have relevance to the group of parents we are considering. As Freud has indicated, the neuroses are characterized by problems associated with an incomplete resolution of the oedipal conflict which occurs in association with the phallic-urethral stage of development. As part of the resolution process, the child makes major advances in establishing role and identity. The characterological features include a growing capacity for group interaction, which is evident in 3- to 6-year-old children. Other characteristic traits are exhibitionism and its opposite, shyness. In group interaction, the child often shows many competitive traits. He may manifest a burning ambition to outstrip others, which is expressed in terms of who has the best or the most, or of who is being included or excluded. At the phallic-urethral level, as at the anal level, we find problems of control, but control is expressed through bossiness and attempts to manage people and not so much through the earlier magic process of identifying and labeling persons and objects. In other words, the child's competitive struggle now is characterized by efforts to direct his energy where he wants it to go. Since part of the control relates to urinating and the differences involved in the sexes, the roles of male and female come to the foreground.

Activity-passivity patterns become associated with the elaboration of male and female identities. Developmentally, this can be observed in the motor-kinesthetic activity seen at this stage. The meaning of this motor activity is to be differentiated from that of the oral phase, where its aim is to obtain primitive gratification. At the phallic-urethral level, motor activity becomes involved in the mastery of sexual phenomena.

The unresolved problems of this phase of development are sometimes apparent in the symptomatology of the delinquent. The classic neurotic delinquent, the mono-symptomatic kleptomaniac, steals some object which symbolically represents an aspect of the phallic-urethral stage of development. A woman, for example, who confines her delinquency to stealing fountain pens, pocket knives, or jewelry, may in this way be expressing her conflict about her male or female identity. In fantasy, sexual identity can only be achieved through the acquisition of a symbol of the genital. This same fantasy may be present in homosexuals; to them male or female identity is thought to be achieved through the incorporation of the male or female genital. However, this component is only one aspect of the problem of homosexuality which is much more complicated and usually includes anal-erotic components as well.

The person who is fixated at the phallic-urethral level has a competitive orientation and ability to direct his energies, which often bring him considerable material success. He is more likely to appear in the newspaper headlines as a questionable operator than to appear voluntarily in social agencies. The wives of these competitive men, however, often seek help with marital problems.

In our caseload, some clients showed mixtures of oral, anal, and phallic-urethral components. Many of the female clients who had problems of phallic-urethral identity complained about the opportunities for personal freedom that are available only to men. The male clients were less likely to express their identity conflict verbally, but tended to reveal it in paradoxical behavior; an alcoholic father, for instance, often took over some of the mothering, cooking, and care of the household when he was sober. Some of the adolescent girls—those who carried knives and were scornful of the "prudes" or "squares" who were not delinquent—seemed to be manifesting both anal-sadistic and phallic-urethral aspects of their personalities.

The treatment process, which we shall describe more fully in the third stage of treatment (Chapter VII), includes helping the client work out his psychosexual problems, especially the identification with the parent of the same sex and the resolution of his hostility to either parent. Presumably treatment should be of somewhat shorter duration than with the other types of character disorders, since these persons are further along in personality organization and do not relate to the therapist in so primitive a fashion.

The Stowe Family

In this family, both parents showed a number of phallic-urethral character traits. Mr. S held a good position as personnel director of a large manufacturing concern. His success in his own field was the result of a delicate balance between a kind of agreeable exhibitionism—a reaction formation against any expression of aggression—and denial of feelings. He chose to live in a suburb where, by comparison with his neighbors, his salary was low; as a result,

61

his wife and children had to cope competitively with families that had more money. He himself denied that he had any wish to compete with his neighbors. Mrs. S showed many of the same traits, although there was more evidence in her of oedipal conflict. She came from a family in which severe, overt, marital problems had been endured for many years. Mrs. S had fled from her conflict about her ambivalent attraction to her brilliant but moody father into an early marriage with a safe man. The marriage, which was based on identification, met many of their symbiotic needs but created problems for the children.

As is true in many attachments of people fixated at the phallic-urethral stage, this couple chose love objects that were like themselves. Mr. and Mrs. S were alike in their use of avoidance and denial techniques, and in their failure to achieve complete sexual identity. Mrs. S, however, was less successful than her husband in her repression of feelings. In general, women who are fixated at this stage give an outward appearance of anal conformity and denial, but soon reveal more fluid emotions than the anal-sadistic group. This becomes apparent in their readier grasp of explanations based on emotional material, and their tendency to give way to tears, of which they are desperately ashamed. The content of the emotional material they divulge has a more clearly oedipal flavor and their problem about identity soon emerges as most important. Mrs. S, like many such clients, did not express a wish for masculinity but was afraid to let herself be completely female. She also related more quickly to the worker than do mothers with anal-sadistic character disorders, and seemed frankly to be looking for an object for identification.

The S boys, Robert and Ralph, who were close in age and just entering adolescence, were exact opposites in every respect. Robert, from infancy, had tended to adopt his father's values and characteristics. Ralph, the younger one, had apparently become the recipient of his parents' negative feelings, including Mrs. S's own repressed delinquent wishes. At 13, Ralph stole large sums of money, dressed like a tough guy, and behaved publicly in ways that offended community mores. The parents reacted with a kind of masochistic endurance and with attempts to conceal their anger and rejection; there was also seductive behavior on the part of the mother. Both parents had a tendency to retreat into illness when pressure became too great.

Treatment of the father began with an effort to help him relax his denial, tolerate some of his own feelings, and understand some of the motivations for Ralph's behavior. It was a slow process, although steady gains were made. One of the problems for the caseworker was the fact that this man, who was intelligent and apparently responsive, showed little carryover from one interview to another as far as understanding was concerned. It also developed that his blind spots made his accounts of happenings at home sound better than they were. While Mr. S was congratulating himself that he and Ralph were becoming more congenial, Ralph would be complaining to his therapist about his feeling of not being wanted at home. Mrs. S's accounts would include some of the father's omissions which would explain Ralph's feelings. However, within the limits of his personality, Mr. S tried hard to carry out the specific recommendations of the clinic.

Mrs. S, whose feelings were closer to the surface, indicated from the start that she felt despair about her inadequacy as a mother and she gave signs of being uncertain about her femininity. She related intensely to the female caseworker with a libidinized kind of identification which was adolescent in quality. She attempted to disguise the homosexual aspects of her feeling by her social manner. The caseworker made no attempt in the early stages to interfere with Mrs. S's defenses and the feeling that was underneath, but utilized the attachment to encourage Mrs. S's female identification and support her in the position of the mother. In this way Mrs. S was enabled to give up some of her managing tendencies and to allow her husband to take a more active role with the boy. She was discouraged from concealing Ralph's misdeeds from her husband as she had formerly done. Although she seemed to feel a certain relief at being able to share responsibility with her husband, she also admitted a feeling of loss at not being free to use her skill in manipulating the family affairs. The caseworker tried to help fill this void by giving her a different conception of her role as a mother. Like her husband, Mrs. S was able to use specific suggestions about practical issues, so long as she had the support of the caseworker.

Mr. S's "forgetting" and his "blind spots" are characteristic repressive mechanisms of persons fixated at the phallic-urethral-oedipal level of development. Although partial repression may co-exist with acting-out symptoms in the character disorders, generally speaking, repression as a mechanism is more characteristic of anxiety or conversion hysteria. Since it is sometimes difficult to distinguish between hysterical symptoms and those of the character disorders, the following summary may be helpful.

Clinical Distinctions

In conversion hysteria, the oedipal conflict is repressed from consciousness and the individual, by the process of introversion, internalizes it. When the conflict threatens to overcome the repression and force its way into consciousness, the ego converts the conflict into a symptom by displacing the conflict onto some body function. For example, in Freud's case of Dora, the girl developed a cough that was like the cough of her father's mistress. The symptom is felt as a discomfort and serves the purpose of keeping the unconscious incestuous wish from consciousness. The hysteric turns to fantasy and to symbolic symptom formation.

The individual with a character disorder does not have the same ability to internalize and contain his conflicts in fantasy or to displace them onto some part of his body. In the main, he acts out the conflict, a process that is the opposite of repression and introversion. In addition, the source of anxiety is not the oedipal conflict, but the earlier trauma of loss of love objects. There is a gradual transition in all these conditions. A person with a character disorder may therefore show some compulsive mechanisms as well as some partial repression. However, to the extent that he is acting out, he is not repressing.

Because of the differences in etiology and resulting personality organization, the treatment approaches must be different in the two instances. The person with hysteria needs to be helped to trace the symptom back to its unconscious source; repressed conflicts as they relate to the unresolved oedipus complex must be uncovered and the associated guilt resolved.

The person with a character disorder requires a very different treatment approach since his superego structure is not sufficiently developed to create guilt. He needs a close relationship with the therapist in order to incorporate an internalized image of a good parent; by internalization, the therapist becomes an ego ideal and a component of the superego. The person needs considerable support in this process of incorporation because of his unresolved depressive nucleus. Attempts at early stages of treatment to deal with his personality problems in terms of guilt, rather than in terms of his infantile needs, are inappropriate and may be one of the reasons for failures in keeping this type of patient in treatment.

After the person has resolved his depressive nucleus and has advanced to the oedipal level of development, a shift in treatment approach may be indicated. The psychic energy, which was devoted to the process of denial and to the repetition compulsions leading to acting-out behavior, becomes available for repressive functions. The person is now able to internalize conflicts and to utilize fantasies instead of acting out his impulses in a primitive way. When the person, through treatment, has reached the phallic-urethral level, the techniques that are applicable to neurotic symptom formations may be used effectively.

Although the phallic-urethral phase of development has received little attention in the literature, some of the manifestations of this stage are familiar to social workers and psychiatrists. These traits occur most often in impulse-ridden persons with character disorders who fall in the category of "mixed type" pathology.

V. The First Stage of Treatment: Establishing a Relationship

SUCCESSFUL CASEWORK TREATMENT of persons with character disorders has long been considered difficult if not impossible. Treatment geared to the defenses of the neurotic and based largely on the technique of clarification is unsuccessful with this group of clients because of the primitive nature of their personality structures. They cannot tolerate the anxiety involved in self-examination. Premature attempts to engage these clients in concentrated work on their "problems" results either in flight or in increased acting out. On the other hand, supportive casework, with the aim of maintaining adaptive patterns, is unsuitable because their adaptive patterns are unsatisfactory both to the individual and to the community. For clients who have character disorders, the goal of casework should be that of promoting gradual maturation with eventual progression toward more advanced levels of personality development. In other words, the growth process, which was interrupted and distorted by trauma or unfavorable milieu, must be resumed and corrected.

The treatment goal cannot be achieved in a few interviews. Treating these clients is a long-term undertaking, involving years of contact geared to each person's special needs and modes of expression. In order to effect any real change in the character structure, the treatment must go through four definite stages: (1) establishing a strong relationship, (2) achieving identification of the client with the caseworker, (3) effecting his emotional separation from the caseworker through establishing the client's own identity, and

(4) helping the client to gain some understanding of his own behavior and its roots in the past. It is not until the fourth stage that clarification can be used in any systematic way.

Treatment that does not operate within the client's developmental structure and the defenses associated with it may actually reinforce the pathology. This may also be true of brief-service contacts in which there are repeated starts and stops, resulting in client behavior that distresses communities and agencies; an example is the chronically dependent client who comes for help in relation to one crisis after another and never resolves the underlying personality problem. However, each stage of treatment that is worked through brings with it some changes in adaptive patterns.

The first stage of treatment, that of establishing a relationship, is perhaps the most difficult one; many cases are lost during this critical period. Contact with a social agency, which mobilizes the client's anxieties about authoritative or parental figures, precipitates a wide range of acting-out behavior. Unless the caseworker understands the meaning of the client's behavior, he cannot respond appropriately. The general and pervasive emotion of these people is fear, although the source of it varies. This fear is not like the universal fear of new situations which, in the case of the neurotic, is soon dissipated by the reality experience of a neutral or friendly response from the caseworker. In the person with a character disorder, the ghosts of old and fearful relationships are not so easily laid. He needs a long experience of testing out the worker—to find out if his worst fears will be realized—before he is free to allow himself to participate in therapeutic communication. Through his ambivalence and fear, he appears to be blocking the very relationship he so desperately seeks.

His fears, as we have mentioned in preceding chapters, may be due to a pathological concept of closeness, involving the threat of death or dissolution, abandonment, rejection, exploitation, control, betrayal, and so forth. The client is constantly on guard to protect himself from the danger that he sees all around him. At the beginning of contact, the caseworker is under far closer scrutiny than the client's disinterested behavior may suggest; no detail of the caseworker's manner, clothing, or actions passes unnoticed. These

67

clients have perfected the skills of sizing up people and "casing the joint." Years later, they often can describe vividly their first impressions of the caseworker and the agency. This sizing up is a form of ego activity by which the client imagines he is transformed from a passive, dependent person into the active, controlling one. As a result, he feels less helpless. This defensive skill frequently leads the observer to ascribe to such a person greater ego strength than actually exists.

Initial Procedures

In approaching a social agency about their delinquent children, parents with character disorders adopt characteristic defensive attitudes. These may include counterattacks on the police, courts, or whatever agency has been involved in their referral; or they may take refuge in silence and play a waiting game. They may accuse themselves abjectly, throwing themselves completely on the mercy of the social worker. They often project the blame for the child's behavior on bad companions or the neighborhood. They may tell of their own severe and sometimes cruel punishment of the child as if to dissociate themselves from his behavior. They may account for the child's delinquency by pointing to their own omissions as if to get ahead of the worker in placing blame. Sometimes they plead guilty to a misdemeanor to avoid punishment for a greater crime. Or they may besiege the caseworker with questions about what they should have done differently.

If the caseworker understands the defensive purpose of these tactics, he will not consider them as major issues in themselves but will respond to them as focal points around which the client's anxiety is mobilized. By listening and expressing sympathy or making other appropriate responses, he can use any one of these defensive maneuvers as a "jumping off" place for further exploration. For instance, if the worker does not cut off the client's complaints about other agencies as simply a defensive projection, he can lead the discussion to recent happenings in the client's life. The client's point of view about these events often contains valuable clues to the role that the present worker would do well to avoid.

The importance of developing communication cannot be overestimated. Communication takes place on several levels, including

68

nonverbal as well as verbal processes. These clients are very quick to notice when the caseworker is bored or tired or fails to recognize them in the waiting-room. On the positive side, spontaneous nonverbal communication, through a raised eyebrow, a shrug, or a grin, is often more convincing to them than words, which they have learned to mistrust. However, one should not neglect the verbal communication. Even if these clients do not appear to listen, it is important to explain to them everything that is going to happen, such as agency procedures and the reasons for them. One must anticipate unexpressed questions, fears, and misgivings by providing answers or by stimulating discussion. One should reply directly to the client's questions and pointed remarks, responding as honestly as possible to the underlying anxiety that they express. It is helpful if the caseworker has some facility with the client's mode of expression, at least to the extent of recognizing its meaning. However, the worker's indiscriminate use of vernacular and especially of "four letter words" may cause trouble, since the client may suspect a trap or be shocked, even when he uses these words himself. To some clients, the use by the worker of "gutter talk" violates their embryonic concept of an ego ideal.

Developmental history of children should be elicited cautiously. Until the parent is comfortable with the caseworker, he may resort to avoidance of details with such statements as, "I don't remember," or "It was normal." Others may give detailed facts about some aspects of the child's life but omit others that hold anxiety for them. Usually the omission or denial is associated with the fear that they have damaged their child in some way. Another area of information, which is likely to be omitted or glossed over, is that of the client's own parental and sibling relationships. Denial and avoidance protect him from the recognition that he received less than another sibling (or thought he did), which may be one of his chief sources of anger and depression. Only when he feels a supporting relationship with the caseworker can he begin to face such painful material. These clients are so pressed by their anxieties that even simple questions may suggest a lack of understanding on the part of the worker. During the early stages of contact, the most urgent question of the parent of a delinquent is often: "Is my child crazy?" or "Am I crazy?" Although the parent may deny this, the child often refers to the clinic as "the nut house."

In the early phase of treatment, much of the worker's activity should take the form of demonstrating certain attitudes. "Acceptance" can be conveyed only by the way one acts toward the client; he will soon know whether he is valued, listened to, and respected as a person, even though he may have to keep testing the worker's attitude for a long time before he will believe it. It is important to show consideration for the client's feelings by apologizing for keeping him waiting (even if he is notoriously lax about time himself), expressing concern about his getting caught in the rain, or sympathizing about the many places he has had to take his child. This consideration should be expressed simply and naturally, since such a client is suspicious of overpoliteness and is quick to brand a person as "a phony." In the beginning, the demonstration of attitudes is essential for establishing contact with the client; in addition, it is laying the groundwork for continuing treatment in which demonstration is to play a vital part. The attitudes which the caseworker should demonstrate are those that he hopes the client will eventually make his own in his relationships with his child and with other people.

At this point, something should be said about the use of authority in casework treatment. Our concept of authority is apt to be a confused one because, as Erich Fromm[1] has said, we fail to distinguish between rational and irrational authority. Rational authority, inherent in the caseworker's role, has its source in competence and is used to help rather than exploit others. It demands neither dictatorial powers nor compliant awe and is of a temporary nature, tending to dissolve itself as the client is able to assume more responsibility for himself. Clients with character disorders, being immature people, are responsive to rational authority once its nature has been amply demonstrated. We shall see, as we go along, that successful casework with many of these clients requires the use of a considerable degree of authority, either implicit or explicit.

Special adaptations of method, geared to understanding the client's psychosexual level of development, are perhaps more im-

[1] Erich Fromm, *Man for Himself*, Rinehart and Co., New York, 1947, p. 9; *The Sane Society*, Rinehart and Co., New York, 1955, p. 95.

portant in the first stage of treatment than in later stages, since it is at the beginning that one either "gets in on the client's wave length" or loses touch with him completely. One of the problems in this first stage, however, is that one has to begin relating in a suitable way even before one has formulated a diagnosis. Therefore, the caseworker must not only use his intellectual understanding of the client's behavior but must develop an intuitive sense about it. In making a diagnosis in a case of this kind, the experienced caseworker learns to depend a great deal on his feelings about the client; he, of course, utilizes social history and observations to check and substantiate his impressions as he goes along.

Although clients with character disorders have certain typical ways of acting which make them readily classifiable, they manifest countless variations that require an individual approach. In other words, although diagnosis is helpful to the caseworker in understanding the client's behavior, it is not in itself a shortcut or a formula for successful therapy. Successes in the past have been due largely to the intuition of perceptive caseworkers. If intuition is supplemented by knowledge, the successes should be more frequent.

Some of the approaches we shall suggest for dealing with parents of delinquents may seem at first to detract from the caseworker's professional role or to negate certain standard casework procedures. This is not our intent. It is our belief that adapting the casework role to the psychological needs of these clients really expands the professional role of caseworkers. The methods proposed here may not be appropriate for use with neurotic clients, for whom other techniques have been developed and tested.

In relation to parents of delinquents, a first principle is that the parent must be "given to" for himself. Such giving is necessary to begin the process of separation of parent and child which is essential for the child's therapy. In dealing with these parents, the caseworker must avoid being put in the position of an anal parent, that is, one who denies dependency needs, and fears that the child (the client) will never "grow up" if he is permitted to regress. In the long run, the casework relationship should mean to the client that he does not have to stay helpless—that it is possible to grow up and still get love.

71

Orally Fixated Parents

In casework with the oral group of parents, one has to keep in mind their impatience for gratification and their tendency to act out their feelings. If a relationship is to be maintained, they must be given something symbolically if not actually. One can offer them concrete help or emotional support with such practical problems as need for medical care, fights with the landlord, or difficulty in obtaining public assistance. Many parents, however, let the caseworker "in on" only a few of these problems until a relationship has been established. This is especially true of oral-erotic clients.

Mrs. Ball, for example, who was mentioned earlier, could talk at first only about her own failures and her childishness. In her early interviews she told of her indulgences in the matter of food, liquor, sex, and spending, as part of her effort to test out the caseworker. Her disregard of the caseworker's offer of help with budgeting (which Mrs. B had mentioned that she needed) was illustrative of the fact that she was not ready to deal with any aspect of her life as a "problem." Also, the caseworker's attempt to have her consider the problem of her obvious underlying "rage" met with the same kind of avoidance. Fortunately, neither attempt by the worker to focus on a problem was so insistent that it caused the client to withdraw. These clients perceive that their problem behavior is indispensable to their emotional economy; they therefore regard any premature attempt to "cure it" as evidence that they are not understood and that the caseworker is not "for" them but "against" them. Eventually, better ways of dealing with their needs can be offered, but for a long time any expression of criticism or disapproval may be interpreted as rejection. Early attempts to question any kind of behavior should be accompanied by unmistakable demonstrations of acceptance.

To maintain an accepting attitude is difficult because these clients continually do things to provoke the caseworker to anger or rejection. Such provocation is part of the repetition-abandonment theme which is repeated whenever they become close to another person. Another theme is their fear of revealing themselves, particularly in early contacts. The worker's reaction to certain types of behavior is tested out in various ways. They may tell detailed stories

72

about the lives of friends, attempting in this oblique manner to discuss something about which they themselves are concerned. If the caseworker recognizes the purpose of telling the story, the incidents can be used to demonstrate attitudes that will help the client tell more about himself. For instance, it was only after Mrs. B had told about the troubles and promiscuity of a girl friend and had elicited sympathy from the caseworker, that she could begin to talk about the "running around" she herself had done. Self-revealment can be encouraged by mentioning to these clients that people often wonder if others would like them if they really knew them. It should be remembered, however, in using this approach that these clients are not sure they want to be liked since affection stirs up their repetitive fear of being abandoned.

One of the most serious problems in working with these parents is their tendency to break appointments. No schedule can be worked out that corresponds with the urgency of their needs. "Demand feeding" is what they would prefer. With Mrs. B, as noted earlier, the first contact with the caseworker stimulated her hope of fulfilment, and so for a few days she felt "lighter." Then her depressive feeling returned, even more painfully, and she resorted to her old mechanisms of denial or substitute gratification. In the early stages of contact with the B family, Mrs. B could sometimes be seen sitting with her dogs in a park near the clinic at the time she had an appointment with the worker. Once Donald telephoned the clinic and left word for Judy to meet Mrs. B in the park, and at other times Judy mentioned the arrangement. When the caseworker became more fully aware of the extent to which Mrs. B's fear of rejection was operating, she decided that the thing to do was to go out and find Mrs. B in the park. (The caseworker in such procedures has to deal with his own fear of rejection.) The caseworker decided that, for Mrs. B, a week's interval between appointments was too long. So, after a few months of contact, the worker said, "I am going to suggest something that may sound funny to you. Since you can't get here once a week, I am going to ask you to come twice." Mrs. B replied, "That doesn't sound funny to me. I always feel better for a few days after I've been here. I might be able to get myself here during that time."

Although Mrs. B never actually kept two appointments a week, she did come more often. In general, it seems wise to vary the arrangement to meet the changing needs of the client. It is unquestionably true, however, that when dealing with clients with oral character disorders one must go much more than half way.

The caseworker usually senses the client's feeling that there is danger in closeness and may feel somewhat uneasy as a result; his uneasiness makes it all the more important for him to convey the fact that he does not share this fear. In other words, he must be careful not to react by trying to prevent the client from telling things about himself. He may limit the time of the interview, but he should not block the client's revelation of anxiety-laden material. To do so would give the client proof that the caseworker considered him unacceptable and unlovable and would confirm his feeling of being misunderstood.

The client's reactions to such interference with his emotional discharge are more difficult to counteract than his reactions to closeness. After an outpouring related to his longing for care or to anger about deprivation or to his own misbehavior, it is usually advisable to prolong the interview a little so that some practical matter can be introduced and some reference can be made to the client's anxiety about the material he has discussed. The caseworker's best insurance against the client's flight from closeness is to "play it cool," that is, not to foster too intense an interaction or to offer too much acceptance. It is important for the caseworker to control his own fantasies of being the completely giving and accepting parent for whom the client has been searching all his life. Living out this fantasy can result only in a regressive situation, possibly inducing the client to act out in ways that will anger and disappoint the caseworker.

Although one does not try to elicit expression of feelings or discussion of them, one can nevertheless "talk to the feelings." In the early phase of the contact, the caseworker may put the feelings into words, saying "some people feel so and so." The client's feelings thereby become more acceptable since they are universal. One can also encourage discussion of reality problems to which feelings are attached. These feelings do not necesssarily have to be verbalized if they are apparent to both caseworker and client. When the client is full of self-accusation, the worker may comment that the client is being harsh with himself, or that we all do things we regret.

But one should be careful not to agree or disagree with the accusation itself.

Since oral-erotic persons in a family operate as a unit, the caseworker must to some extent relate to them as a unit. Even though one works toward the eventual aim of greater individualization of family members, there are many times when the caseworker must have contact with several members of a family. In an agency setting where various family members have separate caseworkers or therapists, there should be some allowance for an impromptu kind of group conference (perhaps in the hall) which these families seem to demand. Here again, some of the general rules that apply to casework with neurotic clients are inappropriate. In dealing with persons with character disorders, a caseworker who sees one member of a family usually has to have more direct contact with other members of the family. This should be recognized as part of the plan, and not considered an unnecessary intrusion.

Parents with oral character disorders can often use more than one social worker, since they have so many needs that require special services. If the social workers operate from a common theoretical base, they are not likely to interfere with each other's efforts, as they might if they were dealing with a neurotic client. In general, these clients are adept at recognizing the differences in professional function, but even if they bring up some of the same problems with each worker, no harm is done. Actually it may be helpful to the client to secure similar responses from two workers. The double reassurance often gives him courage to take some appropriate action.

In the case of Mrs. B, home visits were made occasionally by the leader of the neighborhood club that Judy attended. Athough the group worker had misgivings at first, thinking she might be interfering with Mrs. B's casework treatment, no problems ensued. Mrs. B frequently talked about the same subjects to both workers, but she seemed to be clear about who did what. The two workers kept in touch with each other in a general way, but not in such detail as to make communication a burden. (Co-operation between Judy's therapist and the group worker was more purposefully planned.) Both workers dealing with Mrs. B had a similar orientation to her problem and were clear about each other's roles from the beginning.

75

Sometimes issues came up without warning, but each worker responded in the same way without consulting the other. For instance, Mrs. B suddenly decided that she would not allow Judy to go to camp, complaining that there were boys there. Both workers were aware that Mrs. B's primary reason for objecting was that she could not bear the idea of separation from Judy. Each worker independently dealt patiently with Mrs. B, trying to give her something for herself, emotionally if not literally. The club leader referred to the fact that it was hard to see the children go away, but stressed how much Judy's presence would mean to the other club members. Mrs. B took this as praise of herself and softened noticeably. The caseworker took up the issue from the point of view of Mrs. B, stressing what Mrs. B and the other children could do while Judy was away. She also arranged for money to be provided for Judy's camp clothes.

Work with parents who have oral-sadistic character disorders is difficult because they stir up many negative feelings in the caseworker. Caseworkers have a tendency, in the early phase of contact, to try to placate such a client by securing financial help or special services for them. Since the client's demands (whether explicit or implicit) are expressed in such hostile ways, the worker usually feels that the money or service has been extorted and he naturally resents such tactics. The caseworker is likely to be further annoyed when the client is not appreciative but, instead, seems even more demanding and hostile.

It is important to remember that the need of the oral-sadistic client is, in fact, a bottomless pit and that he is engaged in self-defeating activities which money alone cannot halt. It is true that some of his needs must be met on a realistic basis; however, the caseworker should convey fairly early the nature of the monetary or practical help to be given by the agency. If the worker is clear about the limitations he must set, his resentment does not pile up when the client attempts to force him to give more or when the client succeeds in extracting something. Also, he does not allow this issue of giving or not giving to interfere with treatment. Eventually, he can convey to the client that refusal of requests is not rejection, any more than setting limits with a child is. However, it requires some ingenuity to convey acceptance under these circumstances. One way is for the worker to offer an occasional unsolicited gift or opportunity, which may be a unique experience for a client who is accustomed to wringing reluctant tribute from people and agencies.

At a later stage in treatment, the caseworker must guard against his own resentment if his client seems to come for interviews only when he expects he will be given something. One client herself apologized for this behavior, saying that somehow she could not believe that people liked her unless they proved it by giving her something. At that point, she could be helped to discuss the general problem.

Some home visiting is usually necessary in treating parents with oral character disorders. In addition to the more or less realistic factors of the client's lack of transportation, health handicaps, and the care of many small children, emotional factors may make it difficult to keep office appointments. These parents have such strong fear of rejection and of depression that they avoid helping overtures. Home visits are often indicated in the early phase of treatment, but they should also be used later when a client is inclined to withdraw. In these instances, the home visit is offered as proof of the caseworker's willingness to reach out to the client.

The home visit, like all therapeutic tools, is not a complete answer to a specific problem. It has values and limitations which the caseworker must understand. In visiting, the caseworker must be sensitive to changes in the affect of the client. These changes are often revealed nonverbally and in subtle ways, since the client has little chance for physical withdrawal. To interpret correctly the signs of withdrawal in these clients is not easy. More often than not, the client attempts to get further proof of the worker's interest, even though he may indicate a strong desire to be left alone. Eventually one hopes that the client will reach a point where he will come to the office for at least some of his appointments. But the timing of this goal cannot be arbitrary.

Home visiting, in addition to providing a way to see the client, offers certain technical advantages. An interview in the home often appears to cement the relationship; the worker, after sitting in the family's living-room or kitchen and taking part in their home life, somehow seems closer to the family. One scarcely needs to add that a home visit offers unexcelled opportunity for observing family interaction, but the task of interviewing is more difficult because of the number of persons involved and the many cross-currents of feeling.

Anally Fixated Parents

Since individuals with anal character disorders have personalities that are somewhat better organized than do those who are orally fixated, they can function on a somewhat higher level, can make use of more varied defenses, and do not require such primitive impulse gratification. The hazard for the caseworker who is dealing with the anally fixated lies in the shakiness of their defenses; they become panicky when their control is threatened. The aim of treatment with these people is to help them progress toward developing more secure defenses—of the obsessive compulsive type—so that they can deal with their drives in symbolic ways, that is, through cleanliness rituals and the like instead of acting out. If some anxiety is thus warded off, they will have more ego energy free to deal with reality. Like the orally fixated persons, they also must resume the process of maturing through a secure relationship.

The caseworker immediately runs into the problems created by the client's use of control mechanisms. When a child becomes delinquent, the parent's control over him is threatened, even though the parent may be unconsciously stimulating the delinquency; what the parent really fears is loss of control over his own underlying depression. During periods when the child is acting out, the parent finds denial and projection impossible, and tends to try to use the caseworker or the agency to augment his control by threatening the child or invoking some magic formula for manipulating the child or others. The insistence of the parent upon "rules" can be very annoying. It is important, however, for the caseworker not to rebuff the client by saying, "I cannot help in this way," or "This is your responsibility." One should encourage discussion of realistic alternatives and speculation about possible outcomes. The technique of considering all possibilities, somewhat obsessive in itself, has the value of reinforcing the client's characteristic anal defenses. It may or may not lead to a solution of the practical problem, but it may help to strengthen the client's ego.

If the situation seems to call for some simple concrete advice, one can say that some people find it helpful to do thus and so, leaving the client free to bring up all his objections. The caseworker may give support and encouragement to a parent's ideas or may point out what a child seems to be looking for in the way of control. Often a parent leaves an interview with the expressed intention of handling something in a certain way, but it is a mistake to assume that this is what he will do and to make a reference to it in the next interview. There is a strong chance that he has done something entirely different and that any mention by the caseworker of the earlier plan will be taken as disapproval. Actually the purpose of the discussion was not to help him work out a plan, but to help him begin thinking in a more flexible way. Such a discussion is a way of demonstrating how parents who are not rigidly controlling act toward their children. These clients need the experience of thinking differently in order to become more mature and to be better parents to their children.

Even if the parent's restrictions or punishment of the child seem extreme, it is not wise to encourage him to relax them until he has found some other form of control, such as probation for the child or different controls of his own. If the worker advises him to be more lenient, the parent becomes panicky and, as a defense against depression or to prove that the worker was wrong, may provoke acting out on the part of the child. Also, the child himself may react to the feeling that no one is in control. If the agency is one that can legitimately take control, the worker must be prepared for competition on the part of the parent, and also for his need to prove that "the agency can't handle him either."

If the parent expresses worry about his lack of control of his child, one should not say, "Don't worry." The client should be encouraged to express this worry. This approach has a double advantage; the worker is able to learn something about the nature of the fearful fantasies and is therefore in a better position to help the parent view his situation more realistically. The client also senses the interest and support of the worker. Discussions of this kind should be phrased in terms of events—for instance, "What might happen?" rather than "How do you feel about it?" These persons are fearful of feelings, since these represent weakness and helplessness. Only as the relationship grows are they able to recognize and tolerate feelings.

Quite early in the contact, the parent may try to get the caseworker to take sides between him and the child, or between him and others in some competitive situation he sets up. One should try to avoid taking sides, which can often be done by defining the situation in another way. Above all, one must help the parent "save face" at this stage of treatment. To do so, one must often rescue him from predicaments he gets into by his tendency to issue ultimatums he cannot carry out. For instance, a mother may say that from now on she intends to accompany her son to school to see that he does not truant. The boy resents the plan and retaliates in every way possible; the mother soon finds that she has neither the time nor the energy to carry out her intention. She may, however, cling firmly to the idea that "A mother should carry out threats as well as promises," or "A mother's discipline and control will be lost forever if she backs down." The problem for the caseworker, therefore, is to help the mother renegotiate with her son for some better kind of agreement that is more acceptable to both. The caseworker may have to help her go through this process a number of times before the mother learns not to make wild threats which cause difficulty for her.

One must also help the parent save face in relation to changes in his regulations for the child which are initiated by the child's therapist. For instance, Janet Kane, age 15, complained to her therapist about the lack of spending money. The mother's caseworker undertook to discuss the matter and the mother agreed readily to give the girl an allowance. However, since Janet was ready to believe that everyone cared more for her than did her mother, the caseworker was careful to warn the latter to choose a suitable time to make the new arrangement. It was important to have the mother realize that the clinic was not allied with Janet in her attempts to control her mother.

In the first few contacts, the process of exploration is complicated by the tendency of persons with anal characters to look for "one cause." They both fear and wish that there is only a single cause so that one person can be held responsible. A client of this type feels uneasy about "not knowing" but he is afraid "to know." The caseworker, therefore, should attempt to expand this concept of single causality into one more oriented to reality. This process is a slow one, calling for several approaches. The caseworker must be careful to avoid any activity or comment that the client could interpret as an attempt to fix blame. The social study should be conducted with the client's participation or not at all. The caseworker should explain as fully as possible the reasons for his questions. He should demonstrate and discuss the idea of multiple causality repeatedly. He can do this in a variety of ways—by questioning the client's assumption of single causality, by making generalizations, and by introducing other possible causative factors.

As is evident, the central problem of the parent with an anal character disorder is his confused perception of reality. His own uneasy control of his impulses means that nearly all practical issues are beclouded by his anxiety. He does not perceive what is really happening and he acts on the basis of certain stereotyped ideas. He has a tendency to deal in opposites. The caseworker therefore must be gentle in questioning his concepts of good and bad, all or nothing, and harsh or lenient, which make up his values.

Some of these parents rely heavily on intellectualization, since to them this is an additional form of control. Unless they can explain their feelings, they do not feel comfortable in acting on them. It is important to utilize their defense of intellectualization, although this approach is in no sense a substitute for demonstration. The way one treats the client is, of course, the chief means of demonstrating attitudes, but occasionally there are good opportunities to demonstrate a proper parental approach to the child. The following is an example.

After Janet Kane had run away from an industrial school for the third time and had been missing for several days, her mother (who had an anal sado-masochistic character disorder) telephoned that she had found the girl on a bench at the railroad station. The caseworker went there to meet them and she immediately told Janet that she was glad Janet had been found. She then inquired whether the girl was hungry. Her mother picked up this cue and went to get some food. While Janet was eating, the worker asked what she planned to do now, offering alternatives of returning to the industrial school or of going to the state hospital for observation.

After a good deal of discussion, Janet chose the latter. She wanted to telephone her boy friend before she left the station; her mother was obviously uncertain about letting her do this, but she permitted it. They then went to the clinic to have the commitment paper signed. While this was being done, Janet's mother said to the caseworker, "Today, I learned about living." The worker, surprised, asked, "How?" The mother replied, "I learned you have to go part way with them."

Another use of the medium of demonstration is to convey the idea of unconditional giving. As we have said before, these people are caught at a stage when "being given to" is a reward for meeting certain requirements. Before they can change their ideas about giving and receiving, they must experience something different. Although these people defend their independence vigorously, their dependency needs make trouble for them. The caseworker must give to them, but in ways that will strengthen them and not make them feel weak and helpless. One safe way to give them something is by sharing their concern about physical symptoms and helping them to get the treatment they have neglected because of fears or feelings of worthlessness. Such support can be given in a variety of ways—by expressing concern, by finding out about resources for diagnosis or treatment, by paving the way at the clinic or hospital, or by discussion of the client's fears of anesthesia, surgery, and so forth.

Mrs. Russo, whom we mentioned before, had been extremely resistant for several months, always arriving so late for appointments that there was scarcely time for an interview. She talked chiefly about her son, attempting to find out if he really had broken into her neighbor's house or asking what she was "supposed to do" about his fighting with his older sister. One day she seemed to have trouble breathing and when the worker expressed concern about this, Mrs. R confessed that she suffered at times from sinus trouble and allergies but had not gone to a clinic for fear they would advise an operation on her nose. She told of her fear of anesthetics and how she had nearly died during a tonsillectomy in childhood. She further revealed that her mother had not accompanied her to the hospital, but had sent an older sister. Since it was not possible for the caseworker to go with her to the clinic, she did the next best thing—she offered to telephone a medical social worker who agreed to meet Mrs. R there and talk to the doctor about her condition. Mrs. R was pleased and amazed by this attention. She looked at the caseworker with new friendliness and asked, "Are you a social worker? You mean you're not like 'them'?" By "them" she meant the psychiatrists whom she feared because her brother was in a state hospital. Her whole contact at the child guidance clinic had been charged with feeling about mental illness; underlying her resistance were unverbalized questions about whether her son was crazy like her brother and whether she, too, might become crazy. She had not revealed the extent of her fear of the clinic personnel, and the caseworker had no idea that Mrs. R had questions about her role. In defining one's role with such clients, it is necessary to do it in terms of what one does. Understanding of who one is must come through the experience of the relationship. Mrs. R's recognition of the particular role of the social worker marked the beginning of a new phase of relationship, since it offered her a new possibility for identification.

Sooner or later a mother's demand that her children meet her needs becomes an issue in treatment. The caseworker should in no way minimize the mother's needs, but he should begin slowly to convey to the mother that she expects too much from a child. If there has already been some discussion of the child's feelings and the fact that this acting out is not designed solely to annoy his mother, the caseworker can then begin to help her separate her needs from those of the child. All these ideas must be repeated many times in many different ways.

The process of helping the client to tolerate feelings (his own and those of others) inevitably begins early in the contact, although it should be done cautiously and with sensitivity to the client's threshold of anxiety. Often in the beginning of this process the parent denies knowledge of anything that might have led up to the child's acting out. It may take a good deal of unraveling of details before the parent reveals what it was that touched off the latest battle between them. Even then, in early contacts one cannot interpret the behavior directly. In the period before a relationship is formed, one can only mention that some people feel depressed under certain circumstances or that people, when depressed, are often irritable and strike out at whoever is nearest. This process should go on for a long time with increasing directness.

The parent's fear that the child is "getting away with something" must also be handled on various levels, beginning with a discussion of the fact that the parent is the parent, and that he actually has more power over the child than he thinks because the child needs him in so many ways. This approach is based on the principle that one never takes power or control from these parents without giving them a substitute, either literally or emotionally. Most of these clients feel they are failures as parents. Therefore the statement, "You are the mother," provides them with real reassurance, since it supports the parent's ego.

Most of the above observations about early contacts with parents having anal character disorders apply chiefly to the anal-sadistic group. The anal-erotic group poses some slightly different problems in treatment. With this group, the caseworker must avoid at all costs the appearance of being controlling or easily shocked. If control is necessary, it should come from the court or some other source so that the caseworker can dissociate himself from it. Since these persons are very suspicious, it is important for the caseworker always to be direct and straightforward with them—telephoning other agencies in their presence, letting them see copies of letters written about them, and so forth. Dependency is especially frightening to them because they are so fearful of weakness. The stereotype of femininity, meaning weakness, has to be dissolved for these women before they can move ahead to a mature psychosexual identity. To them, closeness may connote homosexuality, which is another reason for "playing it cool."

Mrs. Carr and Teddy

The following case of Mrs. Carr and her daughter illustrates these observations. Mrs. C asked our help with her 15-year-old daughter, Theodora, nicknamed Teddy, a year or more after she herself had been discharged from prison. She had served a two-year term for a crime which she steadfastly denied, claiming she had been framed. Two older children were married and out of the home. Teddy had been shoplifting and truanting from school. She defied her mother in a variety of ways and embarrassed her by demanding things from her in a way that implied that her mother was stingy with her. Mrs. C blamed the maternal grandmother for Teddy's defiance, since she had kept the girl while the mother was in prison. Mrs. C seemed at the mercy of Teddy, although in every other respect she presented herself as an extremely independent person who could not be controlled. She showed some startling contradictions; although she always worked at masculine jobs, she was small and dainty and came to the clinic dressed in feminine clothes. Teddy wore the typical "half-and-half" uniform of one type of delinquent girl—dungarees topped off with a feminine blouse decorated with a rose.

This case presented an array of problems in management. It was clear from the start that Teddy was in real danger of becoming a serious delinquent because of lack of supervision and control. Not only did her mother work long hours during which Teddy was alone, but her mother's lax attitude about school only served to solidify the truancy. The school authorities were hostile toward the mother, saying that none of her family had ever attended school regularly. Mrs. C could neither part with Teddy nor give her more supervision and companionship. Her long hours of masculine work were a defense against her loneliness, her feeling of being an outcast, and her fear of weakness and helplessness, which were part of her own unsolved problems of identity. Her problems were very much like Teddy's.

The relationship between the two was a mixture of love and hate. To Teddy, Mrs. C was less a mother than a love object; her jealousy was intense toward any man or woman with whom her mother spent any time. The intensity of their relationship was expressed in fighting. The mother found this fighting was preferable to being alone. She was obviously afraid of getting into more trouble. Her fears about her own impulses led her to withdraw from her former friends; she explained this on the basis that, if any of them were observed coming to the house, she would again fall under suspicion. For a time, she had sought companionship at work, going out for beer and pizzas with the young boys, until someone had made a sarcastic comment.

Obviously, no change could be made in the status quo until relationships were formed with both mother and daughter, since no authoritative agency was involved. The caseworker, for the most part, was able to avoid Mrs. C's suspiciousness and fear of being controlled. On one occasion, Mrs. C reported that Teddy had seen part of the clinic report in the guidance office at school. The caseworker immediately read a copy of it to Mrs. C and discussed it with her; this directness seemed to surprise Mrs. C. The two problems that were the most difficult to deal with were the question of Teddy's placement and Mrs. C's fear of closeness. Mrs. C seemed to relate to the worker in spite of her fear. In the early interviews, she tended to withdraw after she had given material about her own family background or her marriage. She later confessed that she suspected that the caseworker's questions meant that she regarded Mrs. C, and not Teddy, as the problem. One problem in which the worker could show interest without frightening Mrs. C was her health.

When Teddy's continued truancy brought a threat of court action, Mrs. C admitted that she had thought of placing her. She said she would do anything rather than face court action again. (Like so many people with character disorders, she was attached to familiar surroundings and had returned to the same town after her release from prison, although she had had chances to "start a new life elsewhere.") Teddy, however, accused her mother of wanting to get rid of her. A plan was evolved for a caseworker from a child-placing agency to get acquainted with Teddy by going with her for some urgent dentistry. Although the imminence of court action seemed to have faded and Mrs. C was again ambivalent about placement, she went along with the plan to the extent of making application at the children's agency. However, the next time she came to the clinic she announced that Teddy had had nine teeth extracted by a dentist whose office was near her sister's house.

After this, Mrs. C began to talk about signs of breast tumor and finally admitted fear of cancer. With encouragement from the worker, she went to a clinic where she was told that she had a gynecological condition which might require a hysterectomy. Mrs. C was extremely upset about the recommendation and talked about wanting to have another baby "the right way"; she meant that during her three previous pregnancies she felt forced to work to support herself and the children and had not allowed her-

86

self to remain in the hospital the required time. It was as if she were still hoping to work out her identity and eventually be a woman and a mother.

Another threat of court action by the school led Mrs. C to withdraw from contact. She suddenly enrolled Teddy in a beauty culture school in another town, removing her from the school's jurisdiction and from the further possibility of clinic attendance. Another factor in Mrs. C's withdrawal must have been her fear of closeness. It seemed as if the strengthening relationship with the caseworker was bringing her perilously close to admitting the crime for which she had been imprisoned and to which she had pleaded "not guilty"; perhaps she also was becoming aware of her infantile homosexual need for a mother. A follow-up contact two and a half years later revealed that Teddy had married and moved to another state with her husband, and that Mrs. C had had a severe illness.

This case illustrates an attempt to work within the framework of the defenses of an anal-erotic mother, by disarming her suspicion with frankness and in no way threatening her independence. We see the typical sequence including a shift to somatic reactions as a means of expressing old hurts, followed by withdrawal which is motivated at least in part by fear of closeness. The plan for placement of Teddy was premature and frightened both the girl and the mother. If we were able to work on this case again, we should not, in the absence of legal authority, urge placement on a voluntary basis.

Illustration of First Stage of Treatment

The casework process of establishing a relationship with an acting-out client is well illustrated in the case of Mrs. Tenney, who during ten years of contact in a family service agency went through all four stages of treatment. She was a Negro woman in her middle thirties, separated from her husband and supporting her 4-year-old adopted son, Dicky, by working as a housekeeper for an invalid woman. In an earlier contact, she had had an intense relationship with a worker for whom she continued to mourn, which added acuteness to her chronic depression and hostility to her usual combativeness. At the time of this later contact she was attending night school, preparatory to studying nursing. Any criticism of the care she gave Dicky touched off a violent temper tantrum and she refused to consider any suggestions about placing him. She maintained the contact with the caseworker through her own initiative, ostensibly consulting her about the crises which arose frequently about Dicky's care. She thought that visiting nurses and nursery school teachers were interfering with her life and she resisted any of their suggestions and manifested considerable provocative hostility toward them.

The process the caseworker adopted was to move along with Mrs. T's defenses without threatening or challenging them. Discussions were focused on the practical issue of helping her to decide whether she could pursue her own career and also be a mother to Dicky. Because her own oral craving for a mother was so intense, it seemed doubtful that she had enough ego strength to work out her underlying depression and be an adequate mother to Dicky. The caseworker believed placement should be the eventual goal.

In retrospect, one can see that Mrs. T had a character disorder of a mixed type, with fixation at both the oral-erotic and anal-erotic levels of psychosexual development. In spite of her oral demands and her provocative hostility, she was extremely likable. She could not show the positive side of her feelings, so she maintained the relationship through hostility. The worker went along with the hostility (and did not try to stop it or "bring it out"), recognizing that the client had need for this kind of control at this time. Mrs. T was obviously bright and she had a dramatic kind of humor which made some of her hostility not too difficult to tolerate.

Early in her relationship with the present worker there was a question of possible suicidal tendencies. When the caseworker suggested that Mrs. T see a psychiatrist, Mrs. T discussed the idea ambivalently, and then acted out the ambivalence. She accepted an appointment with a psychiatrist but immediately thereafter she made complaints about the caseworker both to her employer's daughter and to the caseworker's supervisor. The latter, fortunately, understood the situation and in her conversation with Mrs. T supported the worker. Although the protection of psychiatric advice is needed for client and worker if there is a real question of suicide, the referral at this juncture was ill advised. In instances where the danger of suicide is not great and the client's depression springs from an original infantile loss, the wisest plan is to accept the hostility and stand by. In other words, the caseworker should not allow the client to get rid of him and thus suffer another loss. Actually, a client with a character disorder is not able, in the early stage of treatment, to make use of insight therapy because there is still the need for the preliminary ego-building phase.

The incident did not disrupt the contact and the caseworker continued to focus on the specific practical needs. She insisted on adequate night-time supervision for Dicky, raising the question of possible fears, loneliness, and nightmares, all of which surprised Mrs. T who had regarded fire as the only danger. It was necessary to break down her global concept of danger perceived as a consuming fire into specific items which could be given names and handled realistically. Attempts were also made to help her recognize that Dicky had needs beyond food, shelter, and cleanliness. At the same time, the caseworker made a point of not getting drawn into the concern of other people about Dicky's thinness, trying to convey the idea that there was enough food (love) for Mrs. T and Dicky (both realistically and symbolically). The caseworker was aware that Dicky would not put on much weight because of difficulty in incorporating food (or love). This was also true of Mrs. T, though in a less literal sense. She was inclined to be obese but she could not risk incorporating a new relationship, having been hurt by the loss of one. Although she continued the contact, invariably she compared the caseworker unfavorably to the former one.

Some financial assistance was given at times, which was important symbolically. However, because of the anal-erotic component of the client's character disorder, it had to be given with care. Although Mrs. T's dependency needs were enormous, she could not tolerate thinking of herself as weak. The assistance given was not sufficient to threaten Mrs. T's concept of herself as the breadwinner. Once two dollars was given for a Christmas tree when Mrs. T was depressed and had made no holiday preparations. Help was given with tuition when she decided to return to night school after having given it up, and one week's nursery fee was paid after the timing of payment had aroused a controversy between Mrs. T and the teacher. In each instance, the caseworker offered the help. The nursery fee was paid without Mrs. T's knowledge, which is contrary to usual practice. The caseworker recognized that somehow the issue had to be resolved, since it was interfering with Dicky's care. Mrs. T had always paid reliably before, but she now refused to accede to a new regulation about paying in advance. Actually, the agency's payment of the fee had an unexpected effect on Mrs. T. She found out about it and was both pleased and amused, apparently being able, once she had been given something, to realize that her intransigence was ridiculous and an artifact around which to mobilize her conflicts. Giving Mrs. T money for her tuition had values in strengthening her relationship because it conveyed to her that the worker wanted her needs, as well as Dicky's, to be met. The gift of money for a Christmas tree demonstrated the worker's wish that they be a family and have pleasure together. Gradually, because Mrs. T was receiving something in the contact, she seemed inclined to think more of Dicky and his needs.

The handling of practical problems with these clients is extremely complex because reality issues are so colored by their emotions. In handling such problems, one must be aware of both the practical issue and the associated emotion. The caseworker should be aware that whatever he does will be interpreted symbolically (as the assistance given Mrs. T was interpreted by her). However, he also has a choice about how explicit he wants to to be in handling the emotional factors. The choice depends not only on the depth of the relationship at a particular time, but also on the depth of understanding that the caseworker has of the emotional factors involved.

For instance, a question arose in the early stage of contact with Mrs. T, about how to handle an old venereal infection. The visiting nurse had discovered a notation in an old record which indicated that Mrs. T had perhaps not completed treatment for this condition. Knowing about Mrs. T's outbursts, she was justifiably hesitant about mentioning it to her. The caseworker, knowing that the infection had been mentioned in the social agency record, offered to discuss the question with Mrs. T. It should be noted parenthetically that caseworkers are often asked to take on such responsibility for clients with character disorders. However, it is not always wise to do so. Frequently, it is better to let the world deal its blows. In this instance, it was felt that our contact could stand the strain better than that of the visiting nurse, who was also needed in the situation. Mrs. T took the discussion relatively well and asked the worker to check with the venereal disease clinic.

When it was learned that a spinal puncture would be necessary to determine whether her somewhat irregular treatment had been effective, Mrs. T flatly refused, fearing that she would become paralyzed. What she was saying, in effect, was that if someone really penetrated and saw what was in her, something terrible would happen. The question for the caseworker in such a situation is: To what extent should one deal with an issue as "reality," and to what extent should one express to the client recognition of the destructive forces within him? In this instance, the caseworker did nothing, since it appeared that Mrs. T's relationship with the worker at this time was not strong enough to bear any pressure from the worker without danger of her losing the case entirely.

Mrs. T, herself, was preoccupied with vocational plans, having shifted her ambition from nursing to social work; she was now filled with fantasies about completing high school, college, and social work training. She also planned to continue to care for Dicky. When the caseworker questioned whether she could give him necessary care, Mrs. T accused her of wanting to "pamper" Dicky. Finally, a vocational counselor questioned her educational plans on the basis of age requirements and Mrs. T began searching for a substitute field.

During the time she was trying to complete her high school work, crises about Dicky's care kept arising. Once a neighbor made a complaint to a child-protective agency, reporting that Mrs. T was "abusive" and "a mental case"; the neighbor said she heard Mrs. T curse Dicky in terrible language and threaten to knock him down. She also reported that he was "nervous." Because of the family agency's contact, the SPCC decided not to enter the case. The caseworker, therefore, used the complaint to insist that Dicky needed supervision and should not be allowed to be alone at home. Mrs. T impulsively gave up her job, planning to rely on part-time work. Eventually, she returned to her old job and made plans for Dicky's care. She was surprised when the caseworker suggested that she discuss with Dicky the reasons for her working. At this time she still expressed complete denial of his feelings.

Evidence that Mrs. T was reaching the end of the first stage of treatment was pointed up by Mrs. T's considering going into social work as a profession, as well as by two episodes that demonstrated some capacity for relationship and the beginning incorporation. These occurred after eighteen months of contact. Mr. T's probation officer had visited the home and found the landlady drunk. He had threatened to take Dicky away unless Mrs. T gave up her work and stayed home with the boy. She responded by having one of her violent tantrums. Later she announced to the caseworker that she had too many supervisors. She said, "I will take it from you, but not from anyone else." She then gave up her job, saying that her employer always took her side and gave her advice opposite to that of the worker. In this remark, we see the usual anal dichotomy—the right way versus the wrong way and her way versus the caseworker's way. Immediately after this, the school principal touched off an explosion by telling Mrs. T that Dicky was underweight. Mrs. T kept the school in uproar for a half hour, screaming and yelling in spite of the efforts of the principal and teacher to calm her. In addition to shouting, "I'm salty —I'm a pistol and I go off," she kept saying, "My social worker knows more about children than you ever will."

Although this outburst gave evidence that the relationship had meaning to Mrs. T, it was received with understandable misgivings by the caseworker. To be misquoted noisily in public by a disturbed woman is not exactly good advertising for either a caseworker or an agency. Subsequently there were occasional complaints from people in the community who had gained the impression that the family service agency was supporting Mrs. T financially, and who were indignant about the "misuse of funds." In order to carry such cases, it is necessary that a caseworker feel secure about the agency support of the treatment effort; administrative staff as well as supervisors need to understand thoroughly the difficult process of working with people with character disorders.

Criteria for Measuring the Relationship

The question arises: How does one tell when a relationship has been established? The signs differ with different clients, but one or more of the following actions or attitudes on the part of the

92

client will indicate that there have been some significant gains in the relationship:

A request for help with some reality issue

Evidence of caring about what the caseworker thinks

Quoting the caseworker (either explicitly, "As you said," or implicitly in a dialog with someone else)

Ability to tolerate the caseworker's encouragement to look at reality

A more relaxed and less guarded attitude—possibly venturing some humor

Admission that he could be wrong (even if he doesn't mean it completely)

Entrusting the caseworker with a confidence

Willingness to begin to give background information (which he withheld before)

Coming for appointments more regularly or on time

Any of these signs means that the client has begun to avail himself of the ego-nourishing supply offered by the caseworker, who has tried to convey, "You matter to me," and "You will not be left to cope alone." The shift means that the client has sufficiently relaxed his fears of closeness, trusting, or dependency to begin cautiously to resume the process of growth and maturation through a relationship with a substitute parent figure.

VI. The Second Stage of Treatment: Ego-building through Identification

IN THE SECOND STAGE of treatment the task of ego-strengthening through the client's growing identification with the caseworker becomes the primary casework goal. His previous acting-out behavior, which was designed to test the caseworker, diminishes and the client is better able to tolerate the anxiety of the depression which now comes to the surface as he faces the reality of his situation as well as his own shortcomings. The ego-building process is a gradual one that takes place as the client's identification with the caseworker grows and strengthens. Often the client first expresses his identification through imitation, by trying to dress or act like the caseworker. The process culminates eventually in incorporation of many of the caseworker's attitudes.

This kind of identification, which is transitional in nature, does not bring an end to the problems of relationship; each stage of treatment contains its own transference problems. Although the client allows himself to develop increased dependence on the caseworker in the second stage of treatment, this dependence carries with it in his mind many of the same hazards that have previously been described. The client feels danger in closeness and is fearful of being controlled and possibly exploited, or perhaps being rejected or abandoned. In addition, new problems arise. Some of these are associated with his process of testing out the new ways of functioning he is now learning and of relating them to his usual responses. As a result of such testing he may swing to extremes, acting out at one time and constricting himself at another; in the latter reaction he often utilizes denial. During the early part of this stage of treatment, before the client has developed a strong identification with the caseworker, he may threaten to withdraw from contact. He usually does this when he recognizes that the new methods of behaving, which he observes in the caseworker, may interfere with some of his sources of gratification and with his defenses against anxiety. He senses that he will have to change if he continues the contact. He has no way of knowing that he may find new and more reliable sources of satisfaction if he can learn to postpone immediate gratification of impulses. In instances where the child's acting out is not severe enough to mobilize the anxiety of the parents or of the community, it is often difficult at this stage to keep the parents in treatment. At this point a court order, making treatment a condition of probation, can be of immeasurable help in continuing the casework process.

In oral- or anal-erotic parents, the fear of interruption of gratification may be conscious. They come to realize that continuing treatment will mean that they must struggle against their drinking, misuse of money, sexual promiscuity, and so forth. With anal-sadistic parents, the gratification they fear to lose may be further from consciousness; however, the acting out by the child of their unconscious wishes enables them to maintain their own psychic equilibrium. On a more conscious level, they may perceive that the consequence of a casework relationship may involve allowing the child to grow up, which implies growing up themselves. One extremely hostile and sadistic mother made it clear that she had no intention of continuing contact because she was satisfied with her son the way he was. She said that there had been no recurrence of the shoplifting that had prompted her and the father to seek help. She feared that we would change him from the pleasant, unaggressive boy he was. His difficulty in making real friends, his lack of initiative, and his lack of masculinity were not regarded by her as problems.

If the court does not act as the superego figure for the continuation of treatment, there is little that can be done in certain instances to maintain the contact. If the child is on probation, one can try to have the probation extended. For example, the worker requested the court to extend probation for Judy Ball. Neither the mother nor Judy offered any objection, and both seemed to regard probation as added protection against their impulses. We are inclined to think that continued probation is essential for children of oral-erotic parents, since the latter are so much at the mercy of their self-destructive impulses. In a number of cases, when the court refused to extend probation because there had been no further complaints against the children, the parents withdrew, although there were signs that the children would have liked to continue contact. In one instance it was clear that continued contact with the mother would have meant her having to face the problems of stealing and incest which occurred in her own family when she was a child and which were now recurring in her present family. She previously had blandly denied that an old clinic record on a sibling had anything to do with her family.

As the contact develops, the degree of the client's dependency increases and he may again endeavor to terminate contact. He not only begins to use the relationship but, at the same time, tries to disrupt it by pushing his demands to a point that cannot be tolerated. Frequently, the caseworker and supervisor become frightened and withdraw from the client, not realizing that the excessive dependency in itself is not the important issue, and that it can be used as a step in further growth. In the case of Mrs. Tenney, the caseworker recorded that she thought there was danger of Mrs. T's relying too much on the agency contact and failing to form satisfactory relationships outside. This appraisal did not take into account either Mrs. T's inability to have satisfactory relationships or the nature of the treatment process. The only hope for Mrs. T to develop the capacity to make relationships uncolored by infantile and irrational reactions from the past lay in a long and consistent relationship with a parent figure who could help her grow to a more adult level. Such a relationship can develop only if the caseworker helps the client to incorporate some controls; these controls serve to protect the caseworker from the client's excessive dependency demands and allow him to cope with the client's material. Actually, enough of this process had been actively started with

Mrs. T to allow the contact to continue. The controls set up by the caseworker included: refusal to let Mrs. T work for her; insistence on minimal but realistic safeguards for the care of Dicky (which were always explained as Mrs. T's own wish to care for him); and championing Mrs. T's right to protection, even against herself, and to personal fulfilment.

Understanding the Client's Actions

The T case illustrates the importance of continual awareness on the part of the caseworker of "what is going on" psychologically with the client. It is not always easy to have such understanding of persons whose primary way of expressing their emotions is through action. One summer, during the second stage of treatment, Mrs. T announced that she wanted to go to another city to see her former caseworker, Miss Brooks, with whom she had a continued kind of fantasy relationship, keeping it alive by sending Christmas cards and pictures of Dicky. She said she was afraid that Miss Brooks would be unwilling to see her if the caseworker did not write and give permission for the visit. The caseworker wrote to Miss Brooks and asked that she see Mrs. T, feeling that the two relationships should be brought together in some way because of the ambivalence they perpetuated for Mrs. T.

Actually, Mrs. T's relationship to Miss Brooks had been less that of a client than of a friend. By dealing actively with it, the caseworker was able to bring it into the therapeutic framework. Miss Brooks had a difficult but skilfully conducted interview with Mrs. T who returned feeling that she herself had made a break with her. She had a headache for twenty-four hours, but was pleased that she had not "gone to pieces." She could see that her wish to be housekeeper for Miss Brooks was unrealistic. The caseworker naturally felt some satisfaction that the plan had worked out so well and was not aware, at the time, that it would set off a chain of related events.

Shortly after this incident, Mrs. T began to feel imposed upon by Miss Hobbs, her current employer, and found a pretext to leave or be fired—she was not sure which. After that, she attacked a white woman neighbor who criticized her upbringing of Dicky. The riot squad was called but no action was taken. Thereafter

Mrs. T seemed increasingly depressed and complained of headaches, insomnia, and irregular menstruation. She continued to dwell on her grievances against Miss Hobbs and to imagine ways of getting even with her. She was depressed about Dicky, who stole from her purse, especially when he was angry at her, and who was below average in school achievement. Mrs. T was disappointed in him and saw him only as a hindrance. She said her life seemed at a dead end and she wondered what she would do if she could live it over.

When Dicky left for camp, Mrs. T resumed acquaintance with a white professional man named Arthur, whom she had met two years before in an adult education course in psychology. This time they had an affair. Mrs. T told the caseworker about it in July, threatening to place Dicky in the fall if his presence at home interfered with her educational plans. However, in September she said that she had tapered off the relationship with Arthur before Dicky had returned from camp. She admitted that it had been difficult to make the break and she talked about boarding Dicky and taking training as a practical nurse.

One can trace here a characteristic sequence of behavior. Miss Brooks represented to Mrs. T her first love or only true love. She was identified in a number of ways with an older white man with whom Mrs. T had had her first sexual experience. Both of these people stood for idealized pictures of the missing parents. The purpose of Mrs. T's visit to Miss Brooks was to sort out the fantasy from the reality, much as a placed adolescent girl does when she visits her mother. When Mrs. T returned, disappointed in the fantasy mother, she picked fights with other women. The fighting was followed by somatic reactions (headaches, insomnia, and menstrual difficulties) and the overt sadness of the affective depression. She finally turned to a man for the affection she failed to get from the idealized mother.

Another incident in this sequence was Dicky's stealing. His stealing took place in conjunction with Mrs. T's depression. Some of her anger was vented toward Dicky who now was no longer the magical child who could bring her substitute satisfaction. Her fight with the white woman involved her denial of her Negro heritage, which she felt was responsible for her misfortunes. Her threat to get rid of Dicky represented her wish to get rid of the mother-child relationship which was now so painful to her. But in another way Dicky was the "lost Negro child" (as she put it later) who was herself and whom she could not abandon.

This sequence of behavior—the hypomanic idealized wish, the bitter acting out, and the somatic and affective reactions—should be quickly recognized and handled by the caseworker. He can expect to be caught up in the client's hostility, but he should try to deal with it within the broad diagnostic framework; he should neither react to the hostility nor contribute to it any more than he can help. If one understands what is going on, it is possible to deal with the reactions in emotional terms. In a sense, such handling is a form of clarification, but within a different context from clarification with a neurotic person.

In dealing with clients with character disorders, one endeavors to convey that he understands the emotion, which is usually conscious or partially conscious. Because the client's ego is so weak, he cannot deal with the emotion by himself. The worker, by empathizing with the fear, can give the client the support he needs to experience the emotion rather than to run away from it. The emotion is not ego-alien, as is the case in the neurotic. It does not represent a divergence from his other behavior, but rather is characteristic of his stage of development. The therapeutic effect of letting the client know that his feelings are understood lies both in reducing his sense of isolation and gaining the ego support he needs to begin to limit his acting-out behavior.

Improving the Client's Functioning and his Perception of Reality

In the second stage of treatment of parents, the goal of strengthening the client's ego is usually furthered by the caseworker in two specific ways: (1) by encouraging better functioning as a mother or father and (2) by attempting to improve the client's perception of reality. Although the caseworker always has in mind the well-being of the child, this focus may not be apparent in the content of individual interviews. In treatment of the mother, who is more often available than the father, the caseworker's concern is to help develop a capacity for motherliness. Women with character disorders have failed to reach independence or sexual maturation. The developmental process has been halted at an early level. As has been indicated, these women sometimes can function only as mothers of young babies and actually think of themselves as babies; others act more like siblings or fathers to their children; still others can function as "assistant mothers" only so long as there is an older, more responsible woman on the scene.

The degree to which these women have incorporated maternal capacity depends on their level of psychosexual development. The oral mothers have incorporated the feeding process, but in other areas their maternal identification is inconsistent or precarious. The anal-erotic mothers have identifications with both the mother who feeds and the father who provides. Although they are still in rebellion against orderliness, which they conceive as maternal, they have incorporated some aspects of it in spite of themselves—for instance, they often have sudden and spasmodic attacks of housecleaning and occasional reversion to strictness of discipline. Such responses, which often surprise and confuse them, derive from their identification with their mothers. The anal-sadistic women have incorporated ideals of cleanliness and orderliness, which have become symbols of successful motherhood to them and to which they retreat when their success as mothers comes into question. The more masochistic women have incorporated some of the punishing and disapproving attitudes of their mothers, but not the actual standards. Consequently, they are always worried about what maternal surrogates will think of them, and they want someone else to take over the maternal role. The only way for women with character disorders to become mothers in fact, as well as in name, is for them to continue the interrupted maturation process. Growth in this direction can take place through a casework relationship that is geared to this objective.

The client in this second stage of treatment should be helped to perceive and deal with reality. To the caseworker this may seem like an endlessly repetitious process. In essence, the caseworker provides a corrective parental experience since the child first learns about reality from the adults who care for him. Although the aim of treatment is educational, the process, like any therapy, must take

100

into account the client's defenses and ways of behaving and thinking. The approach to helping clients look at reality should vary according to their needs. Some—especially the oral erotic clients—are unable to consider reality or their own ways of dealing with it except at times of crisis, or not even then, but the caseworker must not desert them in the storm. If the caseworker weathers the storm with them, he often earns the privilege of pointing out the errors in navigation after a safe harbor has been reached.

The technique of verbalizing the person's underlying feelings, as discussed above in relation to Mrs. Tenney, is effective only with clients who have a large oral component in their make-up and whose primitive impulses have undergone little repression. Such persons are aware of feelings that cannot be imagined by those who have achieved greater repression and have developed reaction formations. For instance, when Mrs. Ball assumed that Judy was pregnant and began making plans for the baby, it was obvious that she was motivated by her own unrepressed wish for a baby. When the first pregnancy test was doubtful, it therefore was possible to recognize her ill-concealed regret and discuss with her that the worker knew she wanted a baby very badly, but that it would be better to have a different baby to whom such conflicting emotions would not be attached. Mrs. B discussed this idea in a matter-of-fact way. The worker then suggested that, in the event the second test was negative, Mrs. B should try not to let Judy know that she was disappointed. Mrs. B understood the point and in the next interview her first remark was, "I didn't let Judy know I was disappointed." After the test Mrs. B made a half-hearted attempt to withdraw from contact. Judy let it be known that her mother was in the park directly across from the clinic with the other children, and when the worker went there it was obvious that Mrs. B was hoping she would come.

From mothers who have character disorders of an anal type, the verbalization by the caseworker of the mother's wish to keep the daughter's illegitimate baby is likely to elicit only denial, even though the mother may end up by bringing the baby home from the hospital, completely disregarding any other plan that may have been made with her participation. Keeping the baby represents keeping the infantile part of herself. One such mother later confessed that she had "tried out" the caseworker by talking about girls who had kept their babies, hoping that the worker would express approval. This same mother, who had an anal-erotic character disorder with some paranoid features, repeatedly mentioned drinking and homosexuality in others, but was threatened by the caseworker's gentle suggestion that perhaps there were times when the client herself drank. These brief examples are mentioned to show that the process of separating reality from emotion must be undertaken sensitively and only after a sound relationship has been established.

It is particularly difficult to know when oral clients are ready for realistic discussion of an issue that implies action. Mrs. Ball talked longingly of work during the early contacts, but always in connection with not being wanted anywhere and with her previous difficulties on jobs. It was clear that her talk about work was a way of revealing her self-devaluation and that she was not ready to take any positive action. One day, however, she brought up the subject with slightly different affect, and entered into a discussion of possible employment resources. The caseworker even went so far as to suggest that Mrs. B's present hair-do might prejudice employers against her, since it made her look childish. Mrs. B flushed and looked slightly embarrassed. The subject of work did not come up again for a number of weeks, but suddenly Mrs. B telephoned to say that she was applying to one of the places suggested by the caseworker, and that she had obtained a permanent wave for herself and for Judy. Shortly after this, she succeeded in getting a job in a nursing home where she was successful with the old ladies whom she treated like babies.

Changing Ideas about Others

Treatment of clients with anal-sadistic character disorders requires a more intellectual approach on the part of the worker in helping them to assess reality more accurately. The barrier between thinking and feeling must be broken down in order for such clients to form more realistic concepts about the motivation of other people. Whereas in the first period of treatment the caseworker must make liberal use of generalizations, such as, "Many people feel thus and so," it is now possible to use stories or illustrations about other families or about the caseworker himself. If this device is used too early, it provokes a hostile response since the client has to assert his difference from other persons and deny that the idea applies to him. Before a relationship is established, references to other people are interpreted by the client as an unfavorable comparison of him with his siblings.

In the second stage of treatment, the caseworker can make use of illustrations; he may point out that the feelings the client had as a child were the same as those his child now has. The process is one of helping the client gradually to substitute understanding for his desire for omnipotent control. It should include helping him feel confident as a parent or, in other words, helping him develop an ego ideal. Such reorientation naturally involves some interference with the parent's tendency to depend on his child to meet his needs. In efforts to help the parent understand the child's motivations, one should be careful not to belittle the parent's needs. This somewhat complicated process is illustrated in the following example:

Mrs. Max complained about Ellen's not tidying up her room. "Is that too much to expect?" she asked provocatively. I said, "You don't get results, so it must be. But the question is why?" As we discussed the point, I suggested that in many ways Ellen was not in control of herself and this was why Mrs. M was bringing her to the clinic. Mrs. M looked surprised and said this was true. She guessed she was looking for a quicker cure than was possible. I said it seemed we had not been progressing in the last few weeks because Mrs. M had been trying to control the situation by reasoning and I could not get beyond this point with her. She admitted that this was so and asked why it was. I said I thought that Mrs. M had always tried to handle difficult situations with her head, but this does not work with children. Mrs. M said, "It doesn't work with people."

Later in the interview she referred several times to trying to control things with her head rather than with her heart. I said that only when things were really upset were we able to talk about Mrs. M's feelings. I thought Mrs. M was really very much afraid of her feelings. She went on to talk about Ellen's annoying behavior—not much washing, failing to clean up, and so forth. I talked a little more about how Ellen's feelings interfered with her doing what Mrs. M wants. Finally I used as an example an incident that Mrs. M had described previously. Mrs. M had come home exhausted from shopping and had gone to bed to

103

avoid blowing up at the children. She had explained this to them. Then Ellen got into a fight with Bobby and Mrs. M had to get up to settle it. She scolded Ellen and went back to bed. An hour later Ellen came into her room as if nothing had happened and talked to her affectionately. Mrs. M could not stand it and finally asked her if she didn't have any homework. Ellen had neither done her homework nor tidied up her room, although her mother thought she had had ample time. She was also supposed to have gone to the store. When Mrs. M insisted on the latter, Ellen complained that her mother wanted her to do her homework and then interfered with her doing it. Then there was trouble all over again.

I suggested that we try to see what had happened. I said that Mrs. M had come home tired and cross and had done the sensible thing of trying to get rested. She had explained it to the children. They had understood her (with their heads), but they had felt lonesome and deserted. This made them less able to do things right. Their squabbles irritated Mrs. M more and then she blew up at Ellen, which upset both Mrs. M and Ellen. Ellen went to her room and tried to comfort herself. Finally when she was feeling a little better she came in to reassure herself that Mrs. M was not really angry. Then Mrs. M found that Ellen had not done the simple things that would have pleased her, so they both became angry and each was saying to herself, "She doesn't understand." Mrs. M said with some amazement that she had never thought about how Ellen felt. She remarked that she and Ellen are different. When Ellen gets upset she does nothing; when Mrs. M gets upset she tries to work it off. Laughingly, she said she then "attacks the bureau."

Although such increased self-awareness on the part of Mrs. M might appear to be "insight," it is fragile and transitory and cannot withstand the force of Mrs. M's rage when her infantile needs are not met. Before there can be improvement in her functioning in critical situations, the process of looking at reality with emotional support from the caseworker will have to be repeated many times.

Uncovering a Secret

The case of Mrs. Ward and Roberta, age 14, illustrates how the process of reality testing, including that of "the secret," which is characteristic of clients with character disorders of the sado-masochistic type, is applied to various issues. Roberta had been referred by a nearby boarding school because of stealing, threatening to run away, and extremely provocative behavior. Her adoptive parents had been divorced following the desertion of the adoptive father when Roberta was 4. He had married the woman with whom he had gone away and was living in another city. Roberta, who had been overstimulated by him up to the age of 4, had very ambivalent feelings toward him. Her adoptive mother, who held a responsible business position, lived with her elderly parents in their small home where, after nine years, she still felt like an intruder. The "secret" in this case was Roberta's parentage about which she had not asked because of her adoptive mother's reticent attitude. She had been told only that she was adopted at the age of two months. The following are excerpts from a series of interviews with Mrs. W occurring after a few months of treatment. The first stage of treatment had been brief, since Mrs. W, like many masochistic women, had a strong need for support and had established a relationship quickly. At this time Mrs. W was seen once every two weeks. The repetitiousness of material is characteristic of the second stage of treatment.

September 5. Mrs. W said Roberta could not wait for boarding school to start and had announced that she would not come home on weekends. Mrs. W tried hard not to be hurt. She told Roberta that she would have to come home because otherwise Mrs. W would have to pay extra. I suggested that Roberta really wanted to be wanted and was testing her out. I added that it was better to put it on the basis that Mrs. W wanted her than on that of money. We talked a little about Roberta's insatiable need, which Mrs. W recognized.

At another time recently Mrs. W had said to Roberta during an argument, "What do you really want? If you want to go to your father, it is all right." Roberta had said that she did not want that. I said that Roberta knew that she could not go and she really did not want to. She did not know what she wanted; her wishes were unrealistic and conflicting. I pointed out that Mrs. W could not fulfil them completely and, therefore, Roberta was not grateful for what Mrs. W was doing but was always testing her. I said that helping Roberta would include transforming her wishes into something that could be satisfied by people. In the meantime, we had to try to give her as much emotional support as possible. I pointed out that Mrs. W was the most important person in Roberta's world, although Roberta did not act as if this were so. This apparently had meaning for Mrs. W. I

105

sympathized with the strain Mrs. W was under, especially being in the middle, between Roberta and the grandparents.

September 19. On the day Roberta left for school Mrs. W was hurt by her eagerness to go, but pretended not to notice it. Roberta condescended to wait for breakfast with the family, but talked all the time about school. Suddenly she said to her grandmother, "You fat old thing, sitting there stuffing yourself." Mrs. W considered this behavior inexplicable. I said if we tried to understand it, it might not be so inexplicable. Mrs. W gradually brought out Roberta's fears about a new roommate, the school work, and repeating the grade, but she had not thought these things significant in relation to the way Roberta was acting. I said I thought they caused Roberta uneasiness and uncertainty, which she denied. In addition, she had feelings about leaving the family. I pointed out that Roberta was afraid of tender feelings and that fighting was more comfortable for her than expressing affection. Mrs. W verified the truth of this statement. I added that I thought Roberta's reaction to any kind of tension, including tender feelings and loneliness, was to provoke some kind of fight.

Later, Mrs. W told me that one evening Roberta had suddenly left the TV and had begun to drum loudly on the piano, although her grandfather was trying to sleep. Mrs. W was annoyed and puzzled. I asked what the TV show had been about, but Mrs. W had not been watching it. I suggested that Roberta had reasons for her behavior if we could just detect them. Mrs. W told of Roberta's usual by-play about not coming home weekends, but this time Mrs. W recognized that Roberta always came and would be upset if she were prevented from coming.

Mrs. W expressed her feeling that she was to blame—she had not brought Roberta up right. "They always say it is the parents." I suggested that there were many reasons for Roberta's trouble and perhaps we did not know all of them, but we did know that Roberta lost her father at a very significant time in her life, and before that she had been overstimulated. Mrs. W cried as if with relief, but could not talk about it. Then she asked questions implying that she thought Roberta was hopeless, but that she was afraid to ask. She was always afraid that Roberta would be expelled from school. I pointed out that I was not so alarmed about some of Roberta's behavior as Mrs. W was. It was clear that Roberta had problems, but I thought she could be helped.

For the first time Mrs. W began to ask what therapy really was. I said that in the early stage the important thing was to gain Roberta's confidence, but this was not easy. Later, we would hope to help Roberta figure out more about what she was actually doing and how her behavior made trouble for her but, until she trusted her therapist, it was not possible to do much in this direction. Mrs. W took up the concept of changing and began to apply it to herself. She mentioned her anxiety about driving a car. Once, when she tried to learn from her husband, she nearly injured someone. She asked in an intense way if I drove, as if she were somehow identified with me.

October 3. I went back to something Mrs. W had mentioned about not knowing what to say to Roberta about her father and I asked whether Roberta ever said she wished Mrs. W would remarry. Mrs. W said Roberta had wished that, saying that she had no father. Mrs. W had replied in her literal fashion that of course Roberta had a father and Roberta had made a face. I said, "You know, there's something funny about what you say to Roberta. You seem to recognize her feelings, but then you give her a literal answer which denies them. Perhaps you are afraid of them because they are your own. But what you say puts a barrier between you and Roberta." Mrs. W was interested and we talked a long time about this. I acknowledged that it was difficult to know what to say. She spoke with fear of Roberta's tendency to push Mrs. W into some action. Finally, Mrs. W said thoughtfully that she guessed that she would have to think over all of this.

November 7. When Roberta came home for the weekend, she had rushed into the house, holding out an opened package of cigarettes, saying, "I bought Luckies." Mrs. W said nothing, but the grandmother rose to the bait and expressed horror that Roberta was smoking. Mrs. W made a sign to her to calm down. (We had talked in the previous interview about Roberta's threat to smoke in front of the grandparents. This had led to the subject of Mrs. W's position in the house and her unwillingness to believe how dependent the old people actually were on her. I had questioned why Roberta was smoking and whether it was not just defiance and trying to be big. I had suggested that Mrs. W try not to react, but discuss with Roberta some of the reasons why she wanted to smoke.) Mrs. W inquired about why Roberta's friends had begun to smoke. When Roberta left, she gave Mrs. W the rest of the package.

January 2. Mrs. W complained about Roberta's spending so much time with a young neighbor, Elsie, who had four children. I picked up the undercurrent of hostility and asked how Mrs. W felt about Elsie. She said politely, "I am sure it is nice of her to do all these things for Roberta." When I pressed further about whether Mrs. W would be friendly with Elsie if it were not for Roberta, Mrs. W told of an embarrassing incident when Elsie invited her to the house with Roberta who was so obnoxious that

Elsie's husband sent her home. Mrs. W asked anxiously, "What would you have done?" I said Mrs. W was in a difficult spot. In this situation Roberta had two mothers and was playing one against the other. Mrs. W revealed that she had been conscious of this. She expressed the feeling that she could not control Roberta. She quoted me as saying that she should be more forceful. But if she were to blame, how could she be more forceful? She added that she was not incapable and indecisive about other things. I said I knew she was a capable woman and that Roberta was an extremely difficult child. I suggested that Mrs. W come in next week so that we could go on with this discussion. She seemed deflated and angry, but unable to say so. She said she would come next week if I thought best.

January 9. Mrs. W talked further of Elsie's managing tactics. However, she remarked that she guessed she should be grateful to Elsie. Then she appealed to me, asking, "How should I feel?" I encouraged her to talk more about Elsie. She described Elsie as always doing things for people. The last time she took in some people, her oldest child cried and said that now they would be put out of their beds again. Elsie told Mrs. W that as a child she was like Roberta and, therefore, she understood her. This made Mrs. W feel very inferior. I said it sounded as if Elsie had had problems as a child and still had some. Mrs. W then said that she, herself, was not really incapable and handled a whole department at work. I said Elsie must have problems of her own, and no doubt she handled them in a different way from that of Mrs. W. We talked about the tendency of adolescents to think that everyone knows more than their mothers. I asked if Mrs. W shared any little jokes with Roberta. She looked very surprised and said thoughtfully, "I guess I'm always telling her to pick up something." I pointed out that Mrs. W and Roberta didn't seem to have any fun together and it is important that they should. As Mrs. W rose to go, she said she felt better.

February 6. After some interference by Elsie, Mrs. W had vented some anger to Roberta, saying that she was jealous and had a right to be. I said it was good that Mrs. W could say what she thought. I pointed out that she is Roberta's mother and Roberta has more respect for her when she is able to assert herself. Mrs. W brought out fear of losing control of Roberta. When I commented on this, she said that only once had Roberta actually defied her. She had walked out of the house, but when Mrs. W started out to look for her, she met her coming back. Mrs. W then said that she had never asserted herself, especially with her own parents. I said evidently she thought she was not supposed to have any feelings, but she does have them. She

108

spoke of not wanting to act like a child. I said I was not suggesting that she act like a child, but that she act like a grown-up woman with feelings.

The problem of the "secret" attained significance as Roberta approached her fifteenth birthday and put pressure on her therapist to give her information about her real mother. She refused to ask her adoptive mother. The caseworker brought up the matter with Mrs. W who said at once that Roberta would want to know if she had brothers or sisters and then would go out and look for them. The actual facts were these: the real mother, who was lame from polio, had had two children by her husband and then, after divorcing him, had become pregnant with Roberta. No facts were known about the father. The maternal grandmother, who had assumed responsibility for the two older children, refused to help with the new one.

The worker suggested that there would be less danger of Roberta's acting out this fantasied identification if she knew that her mother had not been a young, unmarried girl. However, Mrs. W seemed to feel that it was impossible to explain the real situation to Roberta. It was too close to her own conflict about sexuality which involved fantasies about promiscuity and incest. She had previously told about a man who had made overtures to her which made her so panicky that she took refuge in flight. Besides, she felt guilty about her own lack of maternal qualities and blamed herself, not only for Roberta's problems, but also for the fact that Roberta had neither father nor siblings. She was not able to verbalize these things but she talked about her fear that Roberta would search for the real mother, whom she presumably would like better. The caseworker discussed with her the feeling, common to so many adoptive parents, that the child's wish to know about the real parents represents rejection of the adoptive parents. Mrs. W accused the worker of raising the issue with Roberta and did not see why Roberta did not ask her if she wanted to know. When the caseworker said that Roberta was afraid of hurting her, Mrs. W said contemptuously that Roberta wasn't afraid of hurting her in other ways. The caseworker said that this issue went deeper. Mrs. W acknowledged that in some respects Roberta did avoid hurting her.

After several interviews on this subject, Mrs. W agreed to tell Roberta what she knew, except about the marriage and the siblings. She invented several things to say which were not known facts, and the caseworker advised her against making any definite statements that she could not back up.

It was soon evident that Mrs. W's "secret" was Roberta's illegitimacy and that our preparatory discussion had loosened up some of Mrs. W's restrictions. When Roberta came home for a weekend, she expressed a wish to see the movie, *Peyton Place,* saying that she had read the book. That evening, Mrs. W, who had previously complained that there was no place in the house to talk to Roberta alone, offered her a snack in the kitchen and yielded to her own curiosity to find out if Roberta had actually read the novel, which she had also read. They had a frank discussion about the illegitimate girl in the story, her mother, and the other girl who was pregnant incestuously. Although no reference was made to Roberta's own background, the way was paved. The talk marked the beginning of a closer relationship between mother and daughter.

Less than a month later Roberta came home in a turbulent and difficult mood. In the course of a quarrel in the bedroom, Mrs. W complained that Roberta made it difficult to talk to her. Mrs. W said she knew Roberta had questions about her real mother, but she didn't give Mrs. W a chance to answer them. Roberta denied that she had any questions, but she came closer and sat on the foot of Mrs. W's bed. Mrs. W told Roberta that because her real mother had been lame she was unable to support her and had had to give her up. Mrs. W said further that the foster family had said that she was the most beautiful baby they had ever boarded. Roberta asked breathlessly, "Did I have any brothers and sisters?" Mrs. W was surprised to find herself saying calmly, "Maybe you did and maybe you didn't." For the moment, at least, Roberta seemed satisfied and now the subject could be opened up again when she felt the need.

Aggression and Sexuality

In the case of the primarily masochistic mother, as typified by Mrs. Kane, the ego-strengthening process of helping the client to look at reality is a slow one. In the beginning it consists of listening and trying to understand. This in itself is therapeutic, since it is a new experience for the client to be listened to in this way. After the fourth interview, Mrs. K commented that the worker always seemed the same. These clients have feelings that are readily accessible to discussion after the helping person has worked his way through some of their fears. For a long time Mrs. K began every interview by quoting hostile remarks about the clinic made by her husband. When these were accepted without retaliation and some undefensive reasons were given for what the clinic was doing, one could feel Mrs. K responding. Since for Mrs. K the prohibited subjects were aggression and sexuality, gradual attempts were made to loosen her restrictions about discussing these topics. She soon began to express some anger against her husband and her own mother, complaining about their attitudes toward sex. She remarked that women who "ran around" seemed to be loved and indulged by their husbands.

The caseworker responded by beginning to handle Mrs. K's "all-or-nothing" systems—asexual versus prostitute, sane versus crazy, and so forth. For instance, there was a considerable discussion of Janet's adolescent sexuality and its difference from adult sexuality. Mrs. K spoke of the difficulty of finding "a middle road," in contrast to the maternal grandmother's "narrow-mindedness." Efforts were also made to help her express appropriate resentment against family members, rather than to let her suppress or distort it. The caseworker always pressed Mrs. K to discuss her insinuations, such as, "Janet was taken away and placed in a better home." She was helped to review what had happened and why. Once when there was confusion about the responsibility of the various agencies with which she had contact, the caseworker agreed that Mrs. K had a right to be angry at being disregarded. It was important to allow her to express justifiable anger rather than to project it. Mrs. K explained that she restricted the freedom of her children in an effort to protect them from broken heads and drowning (the fruits of aggression).

Later, Mrs. K began to demand from her husband more privileges for the older boy, John. She also began to see that she could not control Janet completely, and to recognize that part of Janet wanted to work on the problem, too. In other words, Mrs. K gained some

111

conception of the possibility of the growth of inner control in children. Another aspect of treatment was the effort to help Mrs. K guard against her tendency to let friends and relatives exploit her. She had little ability to say "no."

In such cases, the crisis comes when the client recognizes that the fantasied reward for being good, submissive, and patient is not going to be forthcoming. There is risk then of flight, homicide, suicide, and physical illness. Obviously, at such a time the continued emotional support of the caseworker is essential. In his depressed state, the client will include the caseworker with the ones who "don't care" what becomes of him. He will manifest provocative hostility, a tendency to withdraw, and thinly veiled threats of what he will do to himself. He will confront the caseworker with all the things the caseworker did that turned out badly. The caseworker should try to avoid defensiveness, but not at the expense of concern about the client. He may have to say that he is sorry that something turned out the way it did, but that he had wanted to help the client.

The hostile suffering of the masochistic client in such a critical situation is hard for any caseworker to bear, since the client attempts to drag everyone down with him in his drowning struggle. Eventually the caseworker may become angry and perplexed at being forced to suffer vicariously and may defend himself by saying that the client enjoys suffering and will not extricate himself. This is not strictly true. The client has endured suffering in the past for the reward it was supposed to bring. When the equilibrium of payment and reward is lost, his whole way of life is shattered. With increased depression, he is even less likely to be capable of effective independent action, since dependency has always been one of his major problems. He may have to return, therefore, to the sadistic spouse or the exploiting job, but he should be able to do so under terms that allow him more self-respect. Independence is rarely achieved in one step.

Mrs. K wavered in feelings for several months. At times she felt hopeless about Mr. K and wanted a chance to move out with the children. At other times, she felt that she needed Mr. K to discipline the boys and support the family. Sometimes she would blow up and feel better temporarily. The blowups at this stage of treatment did not give her as much relief as formerly because she no longer believed in the extravagant promises Mr. K made to appease her. One day, when she was violently angry at her husband and irritated by the boys, she "went into a strange state." She spoke to no one but dressed and walked out of the house in a kind of daze. Her report to the caseworker indicated that she feared that a tragedy would occur if she remained in the house. She had a feeling that either Mr. K or she would die violently. At this point she attempted to work out a legal separation, obtain custody of the children, and find housing for the large family. When these efforts proved ineffective, she left a message for the caseworker, "This is the end." She telephoned later blaming the caseworker for everything that had gone wrong with Janet in the past three years. When the caseworker said she was sorry matters had worked out as they had, Mrs. K conceded that the worker had tried to help and apologized for "being mean." Eventually, she returned home, making some stipulations with her husband about management. She soon suffered a recurrence of an old ulcer condition.

In such a crisis situation, the caseworker should not only give emotional support to the client but should take an active part in the client's realistic efforts to change his situation. It is sometimes necessary to make contact with a variety of agencies or resources to supplement the client's efforts in his own behalf. Diagnostically, the important question is whether or not the client's fantasy about the hoped-for reward has shifted or diminished. If the client's activity represents only a new ruse "to bring my husband to his senses," it is better to keep out of it. In the case of an impasse in which the children are suffering, consideration should be given to some form of authoritative action.

Actually, in any work with clients who have character disorders, a good deal of environmental activity on the part of the caseworker is required, at least periodically. In this second stage of treatment, much of the activity may be related to somatic complaints. With the strengthening of the relationship with the caseworker, the client's acting-out behavior may diminish and physical symptoms may develop. Frequently, these symptoms are of long-standing nature, with complicated emotional involvements that must be understood before the client can be helped to make use of facilities for medical treatment.

113

As noted earlier, emotional factors prevented Mrs. Tenney from having the lumbar puncture in the first stage of treatment. During the second stage, she decided to go to a medical clinic for help with menstrual irregularities and to ask for referral to the psychiatric clinic. The caseworker also encouraged her to try to get some clarification of a puzzling genital condition which she described with such vagueness that it was impossible to understand what it was. In connection with the clinic referral, Mrs. T told of her fear of hospitals and related the following story of her mother's death. (This is particularly significant since it was the only historical material that Mrs. T had given to this worker to date.)

> One night, when Mrs. T was 11, her mother had a hemorrhage and became unconscious, after saying, "It's coming." Mrs. T thought something was coming through the window. Her mother was all right for a few days and then went to the hospital for confinement and died. Mrs. T and her grandmother arrived at the hospital fifteen minutes later, unaware that anything was amiss. Mrs. T heard the doctor say that they could have saved the mother but it would have meant tearing the baby apart. She couldn't believe that her mother was dead and tried to get into bed with her.

This revelation is a condensed statement of the client's central problem, such as one is apt to get in the beginning of a contact with a neurotic. Mrs. T's attempt to get in bed with her dead mother represented her wish for reunion with her in death, which became part of her whole self-destructive process. Throughout her life she habitually demanded dependency gratification and then was frightened by it. Only after receiving considerable treatment dealing with her fused feelings about dependency and death could Mrs. T begin to accept her dependency and also the idea of a safe union between mother and child. Her focus on her physical difficulties was a cry for help; she could use them as a way of discharging her feelings of anger and neglect. Her menstrual difficulties served as a means of coping with her fantasies about what a mother does to a daughter and about her relationship with her dead mother. Menstruation, with its bleeding, signified death to her. The fact that the caseworker encouraged Mrs. T to accept referral to the psychiatric clinic and to get medical help for her gynecological problems suggests that the worker had some recognition of the factors involved in her physical symptoms. However, as we shall see, these two aims were premature.

In the course of the physical examination the question of the venereal condition came up. Mrs. T again refused a lumbar puncture and was angry and upset for weeks. Her anger suggests that she believed she had killed her mother by having hostile thoughts about her. She seemed to be trying to put herself in a position where someone was trying to kill her and she reacted by precipitating a fight. At the hospital she continued to press for an appointment with the psychiatrist but in interviews with the caseworker she acted as if the psychiatric referral had been entirely the latter's idea. Once she said to the caseworker that she could not blow up at her because "You are sensitive." When the caseworker laughed, saying that this was one place where it was safe to blow up, Mrs. T said, "You are the only one I don't want to keep out of my business."

Mrs. T was seen by a woman psychiatrist and began to relate positively to her until the latter heard about the venereal condition. According to Mrs. T, the psychiatrist then refused to see her again until she had had the lumbar puncture. Mrs. T did not return to the psychiatrist, although she had the puncture a short time later on her own initiative, after vainly trying to force the caseworker to order her to have it. The caseworker discussed the pros and cons with Mrs. T and conveyed her wish that Mrs. T would have it done, but she never told her expicitly to do so. Mrs. T therefore did not have to oppose her and could use the caseworker's reasoning as her own. This technique was characteristic of the handling of a number of issues during the second period and is typical of the way an anal-erotic client can be handled.

Questions about Placement of Children

Another reality issue that frequently presents difficulties in the second stage of treatment of the parent of a delinquent child is the question of placement for a child. Unless placement is ordered by the court, the caseworker finds himself in a difficult position because of the parent's ambivalence. This ambivalence emerges even when the parent has asked for placement with great urgency. For instance, when Mrs. Ball asked for placement of Judy at the height of the incest excitement, her attitude was that of "If thine hand offend thee, cut it off." Placement was also her only way of flight from a situation that made her feel utterly helpless. Only a few weeks later Mrs. B was reluctant to let Judy go to camp, indicating that the girl had been re-incorporated into the close family group.

In the fall, under pressure from Judy's therapist, the caseworker reopened the placement issue, presenting it as a recommendation with the force of professional authority. The result was that Mrs. B managed to elude the caseworker, even when home visits were made. She would leave the downstairs door locked (there was no bell) or she would "just happen" to be out. At this time she relegated the caseworker to the role of the mean, cruel grandmother (who had given away her daughter's children) and placed Judy's therapist in the role of the beautiful, young, lost mother—telling her all her troubles by telephone. It was six months or more before the caseworker, using whatever chance opportunities were offered, was able to convince her that the clinic would not place Judy against Mrs. B's wishes. Only then did she begin to relate as formerly.

Some of the parents with anal character disorders express their ambivalence about placement by an on-again off-again attitude. Such a parent will insist on placement until it is offered and then oppose it completely and seduce the child into giving up the idea, if he has begun to show interest in it. There may be a number of factors influencing the parent to hold on to the child, such as his need for the child to act out his own repressed conflicts, fear of loss of the child as love object (a feeling that is both sadistic and masochistic), and guilt about failure as a parent. Frequently the desire to keep the child is related to the parent's own feelings about childhood placements and a childhood resolution that he would never do this to his own child.

The referral of Joey Finn, age 6, by a family service agency, indicated obvious need for his removal from his adoptive home. The complaints of his adoptive mother, the neighbors, and the landlord included fire setting, stealing (money and large amounts of food), destructiveness, wetting, soiling, and defiance. Mr. and Mrs. F had taken Joey to board when he was 14 months old and had adopted him legally at 3 years; his real parents had disappeared.

Mr. and Mrs. F had previously been refused a child by an adoption agency on the basis that Mrs. F was very immature and had not worked out any of the problems resulting from her own upset childhood. Her parents had separated when she was 4. She had lived with her father in a variety of makeshift arrangements while her younger brother had remained with the mother. Her father remarried and, when she was 7, he was sent to jail; her stepmother then took her back to her mother. Her mother, who later was diagnosed as mentally disturbed (paranoid), was unable to handle her. She was placed and returned home several times. The last placement, in adolescence, was in a girls' reformatory. She married Mr. F at a time when she was suffering from a number of physical symptoms and seemed unable to keep a job. Mr. F also felt neglected and homeless, having left home after a fight with his mother who, he thought, preferred his brothers. After a miscarriage, Mrs. F began to try to adopt children and then took Joey to board. When he was 2, she had a complete hysterectomy which left her nervous and depressed.

Joey was described as being too quiet as a baby and Mrs. F used to try to "stir him up." However, when he was 3 or 4 he went "hog wild." This was after a series of traumas—circumcision, a tonsillectomy, the unexpected placement in the family of a 2-week-old baby, Joan. Mrs. F became completely wrapped up in the new baby whom she subsequently adopted.

When seen in the clinic, Joey was an attractive, bright, and extremely overactive youngster. Testing was accomplished only through the perseverance and flexibility of the psychologist who, for instance, followed Joey under the table and continued the testing there. The diagnostic study, including a neurological check-up as well as a physical examination, was interrupted more than once by broken appointments. Both Joey and Joan had communicable diseases during this period, but there were other less plausible excuses. In the meantime, Joey's activities, which had aroused the ire of neighbors, appeared to have died down and, with them, his mother's concern.

At the end of the study, while we were awaiting the results of the medical tests, his mother telephoned frantically, saying, "Something has to be done." Joey had started a fire in a neighbor's yard and

117

the landlord was threatening to evict them. The school was considering expelling him because he was so uncontrollable. Mrs. F made it clear that placement was the only thing possible. However, Christmas intervened and when we saw her two weeks later she did did not want placement, saying that she was attached to Joey and that he was nice, clean, and affectionate. She added that he was trying to be good.

In the early months of treatment, Mrs. F, in the way characteristic of persons with anal character disorders, was preoccupied with finding "one cause" for his behavior and "one remedy." Discussion brought out Joey's fascination with guns, his compulsive hitting of Joan, and his fights with other children. It became clear that he had a strong need to provoke punishment. The contact then lapsed for two months, in spite of letters and telephone calls.

When Mrs. F returned, she said she was ready to kill Joey. He had frightened her by disappearing for several hours, had played in the mud in his Easter suit, and the school was again threatening to expel him. She said he was hopeless and she was giving up. The caseworker said that the clinic had no chance to help her when she stayed away. Mrs. F tried to avoid the issue but, when pressed, she said that she had been fighting with her husband and had finally locked him out of the house. After three days, the priest convinced her that they were both wrong and she had agreed to try again. She had been afraid to tell anyone about the fighting for fear the children would be taken away. She said she could not bear to place Joey because of her own childhood experiences.

She expressed anger at Joey for being "unreasonable and unreachable." She started to blame his faults on heredity and then corrected herself, saying, "I am bad for him." She said she gave in to him and kept Mr. F from punishing him. She ended by saying that she did not understand him. After the caseworker talked a little about the difficulty of understanding a child, Mrs. F seemed relieved. The caseworker said that it might be necessary to consider temporary placement of Joey at some time, but that, with or without it, the clinic wanted to help all four of them. At this point, Mrs. F's resistance to placement was strong and, in addition, there was the real problem of where one could place a child of this age with such severe acting-out problems.

Subsequently Mrs. F talked more freely about her marital problems and her handling of Joey. She often felt paralyzed by her fear of acting like her own mother and she had no other pattern to follow. A few months later, she decided that the marital situation was hopeless and she moved out of the house, taking the children and most of the furniture with her. She had told the caseworker, in advance, that she was going to do this but she made it clear that she was not asking advice. She had already obtained legal advice.

After this sudden separation, we continued to see Mr. F, as well as Mrs. F. Mrs. F obtained a separation agreement and showed no signs of returning to her husband, although she did express some guilt about the way she had left him and some sympathy for him. She found it difficult to live on the money he paid her and she insisted on taking a job, against the advice of everyone. Joey wore out sitters and caretakers very rapidly, and the new school threatened to expel him. Mrs. F expressed fear of killing him when she was angry. She said she wanted to place him somewhere where he would get treatment and then have him returned to her. She had a great deal of anxiety about not getting him back. She tried staying home from work, but then reported, with a slightly "I told you so" attitude, that Joey was just as bad as ever. She complained about his destructiveness and about his messing his pants. She said she had made a mess of her life—she shouldn't have taken the children. Anyone else could have given them more. She described her unavailing efforts to get love from her mother, Mr. F, and her brother. She had now begun to search for her missing father.

During this period Mrs. F was referred to a child-placement agency which had trouble in finding any placement facility for Joey. He was finally placed on trial in a small, homelike boarding school where he adjusted better than might have been anticipated. Although Mrs. F had agreed to keep in touch with the caseworker, she found reasons for not keeping appointments. Her contact with the children's agency continued on a minimal basis. Joey continued in the boarding school which, unfortunately, made it impossible for him to secure the therapy he needed. However, the need for environmental stability was urgent at this juncture.

Mrs. F is one of the mothers with whom it is virtually impossible to keep a contact without the motivating force of authority or anxiety. When there is no court requirement in such a case, the clinic or agency, after making clear the wish to help, can only wait for another crisis which will bring the client back. If the relationship is potentially good, it can be resumed with very little loss. In fact, the client, during the period when the case is "closed," may be thinking about the contact and acting on ideas that he has absorbed. Many contacts which, from the agency point of view, are "intermittent," have more continuity in the client's mind than the caseworker imagines.

Gains in Second Stage of Treatment

Even the client who discontinues contact in the second stage of treatment may have incorporated some of the caseworker's attitudes or ways of handling certain situations. He may have made some progress toward maturation. For instance, Mrs. Ball during this period quoted herself as saying to her employer at the nursing home, "Of course I'll be in. I've always said that when you take a job, you have a responsibility to come." The caseworker smiled and said, "You've always said it, but you couldn't always do it." With a kind of shy, sideways glance Mrs. B replied, "I've grown up, too." In view of the irregular contact and all the problems surrounding it, the growth on the part of Mrs. B, which had been noted by various therapists at the clinic, suggests that improvement does not necessarily depend upon the regularity with which the parent is seen. In a family in which the mother has an oral-erotic character disorder, treatment—like everything else—is shared by all family members.

Whether or not any maturation occurs in the parent, the relationship with the caseworker at least has the effect of diverting his needs away from the child and they therefore interfere less with the child's therapy and growth. In the case of Mrs. Park, the relationship had this value. Her teenage son, Kenneth, had stolen large sums of money, but court action was averted by the parents' willingness to make repayment. Kenneth's problem lay chiefly in his search for identity. His mother's seductiveness and her smoldering resentment against his father made it hard for him to achieve male identification. Mrs. P, who had an anal-erotic character disorder bordering on the psychotic, formed an intense relationship with the caseworker, which left Kenneth free to form a closer relationship with his father. Treatment with Mrs. P terminated in the second phase. At that time Kenneth was no longer engaged in thefts and he himself did not wish to continue contact. Also, Mrs. P had become afraid of her homosexual feelings and of her hostile feelings toward her husband; she seemed to feel that voicing her complaints against him required that she take action about leaving him, which she was not ready to do. Follow-up contacts over a period of two years, however, showed that Kenneth's improvement had continued.

The second stage of treatment with these parents, if it progresses satisfactorily, is one in which the caseworker uses the relationship to help the client resume the maturation process which had been arrested in early childhood. The goal is primarily that of strengthening the ego; the techniques include demonstrating new attitudes, helping the client to develop some controls, and dealing with misconceptions that interfere with his ability to perceive reality factors. Diagnostically, it is essential for the caseworker to know what point the client has reached in his psychosexual development and what his behavior signifies. If the parent is helped toward maturation and to achieve better reality orientation, considerable benefit obviously will accrue to his children.

One word of caution should be added. Although parents may achieve gains during this second stage of treatment which may be lasting, one should not be too hasty in making a positive evaluation of the treatment. Some clients, through a pseudo-identification with the caseworker, show a lessening of symptoms but this improvement may not hold up after the discontinuance of contact. The change may in reality be a temporary "transference cure." In other instances, a parent with an oral character disorder may begin to show some anal character traits. Although such change is an indication of progress, it does not mean that he will be able to solve his problems or those of his children in an adult way. For instance, Mrs. Ball, after she had expressed satisfaction at having "grown up" enough to work regularly, talked again of her own childishness and of her fear of being unable to deal with her children's teenage problems.

VII. The Third Stage of Treatment: Helping the Client Establish a Separate Identity

THE CHIEF AIM of the third stage of treatment is to help the client establish a separate identity. This phase of treatment is least familiar to caseworkers and, in consequence, the techniques for dealing with the client's behavior are not too adequately formulated. One reason for the lag is the fact that cases are frequently closed during the second stage because of a misleading "transference cure" or because the symptoms are not understood and are interpreted as regression. A clearer understanding of the dynamics would often result in cases being carried through to the fourth stage, thus providing opportunity for the client to achieve basic personality change.

The technical problem in the third stage of treatment is that of understanding and handling the client's efforts to separate himself from the caseworker. The client has gradually developed identification with the worker and has begun to use some of the latter's methods for dealing with reality. As he does so, he turns against the worker and often reverts to earlier patterns of behavior. This apparent regression is likely to discourage and frighten the worker if he does not realize what is happening. Actually this process of separation resembles the process of the adolescent separating from the parent. It involves similar depression, anxiety, hostility, and search for identity. As Helene Deutsch says, "No emotional tie is given up without the accompaniment of negative feelings; and in

122

the child's primitive emotional life, dependence is always identical with love, and the struggle for independence is accompanied by hostility. This struggle must use the negative feelings to overcome the mother tie and the fear of losing her. Thus, the infantile anxieties of the period of the struggle for liberation stem from two sources—from the aggression that is used to achieve this liberation, and from the fear of losing the mother." [1]

If the caseworker recognizes the process of separation, he can convey to the client the feeling that his hostility is not reciprocated and that the worker will support him in his efforts to grow up and act independently. An added complication lies in the fact that, in adult clients, the separation process may be accompanied by severe depression. The depression obviously stems from the prospect of loss but, with these clients, it may appear more severe because they have given up some of their usual ways—their acting-out behavior—of dealing with their chronic depression. At this stage their feelings of depression are no longer hidden from themselves or the worker.

This third stage of treatment parallels the adolescent period of development in a number of ways. Both are marked by an intense search for identity with accompanying extremes of emotion and a tendency toward regression. Also, adolescence is characterized by a revival of oedipal struggles involving both homosexual and heterosexual strivings. Persons with character disorders, however, are strongly fixated at the pregenital level and, unless pregenital problems are worked through, these clients do not achieve a resolution of the oedipal conflict and reach a phase of development marked by neurotic rather than acting-out expressions of their instinctual strivings.

Analysis of the Tenney Case

The case of Mrs. Tenney, mentioned previously, illustrates the dynamics at work in the third stage of treatment. This case was studied in the delinquency research unit of the Judge Baker Guidance Center in order to test our theories about the various stages of treatment. The casework service was given in a family service

---

[1] Helene Deutsch, M.D., *The Psychology of Women*, Grune and Stratton, New York, 1944, Vol. 1, pp. 243–244.

agency and covered a period of ten years. The stages of treatment were readily identifiable although the caseworker had had no such formulation in mind while working on the case. The first period of treatment, that of forming a relationship, had taken eighteen months, with a good deal of acting out on Mrs. T's part. The second stage, that of developing identification with the caseworker, had lasted thirty months. During the second stage, Mrs. T had calmed down considerably and handled her relationships with Dicky and the outside world in a more constructive way. The third stage, which will now be discussed, lasted thirty months. The same caseworker treated Mrs. T through all four stages of treatment. Mention has been made of an earlier contact with another caseworker, Miss Brooks.

The following is a brief history of this client:

Mrs. T, a Negro, was 38 years old at the beginning of the third stage of treatment. Dicky was then 8. Mrs. T's mother, who was very young when Mrs. T was born, never left her own mother; the latter acted as a substitute mother for Mrs. T. Mrs. T's father deserted, reappearing occasionally. He died when Mrs. T was 6. Her mother remarried and died in childbirth when Mrs. T was 11. Her grandmother died a year later. An aunt kept Mrs. T until the insurance money ran out and then turned her over to her stepfather; he found her difficult to handle and boarded her with various individuals. Beginning at the age of 16, she was placed by a children's agency in a series of work homes where she was often intractable and defiant. She told the children's agency that before her stepfather's remarriage, which occurred when she was 14, she had had frequent sexual relations with him; physical examination, however, showed no penetration. Whether or not there was actual physical contact, she had obviously sexualized the relationship. While under the care of the children's agency, she became involved with an older, white man, George. He was a lawyer and a relative of the mother of one of the families for whom she worked. Mrs. T later spoke devotedly of this family, stating that she left this home because she was the only Negro girl in the neighborhood and had no companions. She married Mr. T a number of years later, at the age of 27.

(The sparseness of the history, at this point, is not accidental. Not until Mrs. T had established a real relationship could she trust anyone with the details that were most fraught with meaning. For instance, it was not until much later that the caseworker learned that Mrs. T's grandmother was white, a daughter of a German man and a woman who was partly Indian. Similarly, the years between Mrs. T's leaving the work home and her marriage were left blank.)

During her first year of marriage, she was admitted to a hospital with a diagnosis of pregnancy, but signed herself out after a few days and never had a baby. Later, she took Dicky, a seriously undernourished infant of a few weeks into her home, together with his mother, a notoriously promiscuous woman whose other children had been taken from her because of neglect. Rumor had it that Mr. T was the father of this baby. Mrs. T managed to keep the baby and get rid of the mother. She adopted Dicky legally, concealing from agencies her belief that Mr. T was his father.

Mrs. T worked very hard to nourish the neglected baby, saying later that she did everything but give birth to him. After her separation from Mr. T she placed Dicky in a nursery school and went to work, at the same time taking night courses to complete her high school education with the hope of going on to some kind of professional training. Whenever Dicky's illness or physical care interfered with these plans, she was angry and frustrated, but she would never consider placement. During the first two stages of treatment, the contact consisted largely of efforts to help her to gain some personal satisfactions and still be a good mother to Dicky.

In these earlier contacts, certain repetitious trends in Mrs. T's behavior were observable: (1) Her search for substitute parental figures, her tendency to take in neglected children, and her wish for a baby of her own. (2) Her search for identity, expressed in questions about race and in attempts to imitate people around her. She used primitive mechanisms of direct imitation and incorporation, which precede the oedipal level of development. The imitation often resulted in a caricature of the model. (3) Her childish ways of relating to people. These involved: (a) playing one person against another; (b) alternately presenting herself as an object of pity and being scornful of people for not knowing anything; and (c) manipulating people for her own ends. Her observations of people were shrewd and acute; she had a good memory for their remarks or actions and a tendency to mimic or ridicule them. These traits, which are characteristic of persons with anal-erotic character disorders, stem from their preoccupation during childhood with the words and action of the grownups, in the hope of finding out the secrets that the grownups are keeping from them.

Diagnostically, Mrs. T's character disorder would be classified as a mixed type. She had characteristics of the oral and anal stages of psychosexual development as well as a few manifestations of infantile hysteria—for example, the incident of the pseudo-pregnancy. Her character structure, however, was fixated mainly at preoedipal levels, as evidenced in her insistent demands associated with her unresolved oral needs. She expressed these needs in repeated references to rejection and abandonment; at times when her needs were not met, she manifested depressed feelings. When depressed, she withdrew, felt unlovable, and ate excessively, gaining weight rapidly. The strong anal-erotic component was apparent in her delight in rebellion and messiness, as well as in her bisexuality, her feeling of omnipotence, her need to control, and her marked ambivalence. (It is our belief that persons with mixed character disorders are more readily treatable than those fixated at one level of preoedipal development. Persons of mixed types have at their disposal more ways of relating to others. Also, their egos are more flexible and better developed.)

Early Attitudes in the Third Phase

The beginning of the third stage of treatment with Mrs. T was marked by her increased independence, shown in wanting less frequent appointments and in her expressed intention of helping herself by reading popular articles on personality adjustment. She denied the value of the agency contact, saying that she had used her contacts with social workers mainly as a means of improving herself, that is, using the workers as models for dress and manners. She showed less anxiety about the caseworker's approaching vacation than she ever had before. She asserted herself by signing Mr. T's name to Dicky's report card "to keep the school out of my business." This was an expression of the male part of herself which, in her mind, was equated with independence in contrast to the female part which she regarded as dependent and helpless.

When the caseworker returned from an early summer vacation, Mrs. T announced that she was going to pay for Dicky's camp herself. She told of increased activity in the PTA and of punishing

Dicky severely for his negative attitude toward school. She had refused to let him use his bicycle until his grades and conduct improved and she remained adamant even after he had run away and had been found hiding in the cellar late at night. Her siding with the authority of the school, rather than against it, and her punishment of Dicky suggest that she had given up some of her anal-erotic rebellion and had moved into the anal-sadistic phase. Her attitudes reflected the usual extreme swing of the pendulum.

Only after she had related all these occurrences did she tell the caseworker that her white friend, Arthur, had been killed in an automobile accident. She showed minimal affect, saying only that she was glad she had not been with him when the collision occurred, but subsequently her behavior revealed the degree of her depression. She began coming to the office only once a month. She was angry at Dicky who was reacting to her mood with inability to learn at school; he began filling his time with sports and club activities and was rarely home. Her ambivalence about their being together was evident in her fear that his father would somehow reappear and take him away and in her threats to Dicky that she might die and he would then be sent back to his real mother. She said she really wanted a baby of her own because "a mother's feeling is what counts." She began to talk about ultimately running a children's home or camp and made plans to take courses in quantity cooking.

In the fall, she reported that she cried a lot at home. The worker offered to see her every other week for a time. She revealed that after Arthur's death she had thought she was pregnant, but had been afraid to tell the caseworker for two reasons: because the caseworker would insist on tests which would reveal that she was not pregnant, and because she was uncertain that the caseworker would stand by her if she were. She brought out her conflict between her wish for a baby and her guilt, fear, and shame if she had one. It was clarified that she wanted a white baby. She said that she had been trying to relate to a Negro group because she thought the caseworker wished it. The caseworker said that it was not she, but part of Mrs. T, who wished it. They talked about ways of finding a mixed group. Mrs. T brought in magazines with articles on psychiatry, a story of Ethel Waters' life, and so forth, and discussed them in relation to herself. She wondered if she were in the menopause or going crazy, but resisted any suggestion of a psychiatric clinic. She said the caseworker helped her because she never fought with her, even when she had tantrums. She mentioned again some concern about her genitals, but without making the difficulty any clearer.

It happened that Ethel Waters was in town playing in *Member of the Wedding* at a time when Mrs. T was especially pressed for money. Knowing how much Mrs. T wanted to see her, the caseworker offered her money to buy a ticket. Mrs. T later said this was one of the best things the caseworker had ever done for her. At the time, Mrs. T was surprised to find that her identification was not with Bernice, the mature woman played by Ethel Waters, but with the adolescent girl, Frankie, who wanted so much to be included in her brother's marriage.

In this material she was expressing the magical connection she had made between birth and death; she was endeavoring to deal with her fear of death through fantasies of pregnancy. Her loss of Arthur was a re-enactment of her loss of her mother. In trying to handle the accompanying depression, she assumed all the possible roles—the child who is lost, the mother who is lost (by withdrawing from Dicky), and the wish to care for one child or many children. Although her behavior at this time was regressive, the regression did not indicate a failure in treatment; rather, it was a necessary phase for the resolution of the underlying depression. Her typical responses recurred under stress; at this stage of treatment, the source of depression can be expressed by the client more directly. Such responses, however, can create considerable anxiety in the caseworker, who becomes concerned both about the client's depression and about the possibility of her acting out the fantasies about having a baby. In this case the only possible course for the caseworker to follow was to stand by and try to help Mrs. T work through the fantasy in her feeling of kinship to "Frankie." It was clear that she was reaching the adolescent level of development.

Meanwhile Mrs. T's efforts to go to cooking school met with delays. She refused the suggestion of a vocational adviser that she learn on a job. The caseworker recognized dimly that Mrs. T, because of her regression, was unable to cope with the realities of a new job and did not urge her to take one. Mrs. T began to fill her time by befriending unfortunate Negroes. The battle for control with Dicky continued. She would allude to her sadistic punishment of him as if to defy the caseworker to interfere. Mrs. T at this time exerted strong pressure on her caseworker to assume treatment of Dicky, to replace Mr. F, who had been treating him. She insisted that Dicky came to the office only in hope of catching a glimpse of her caseworker. This pressure continued for many months and the caseworker was mystified by it.

In retrospect, it seemed clear that Mrs. T, who was struggling with adolescent problems, was searching desperately to establish her own identity. This search was colored by her anality, involving choices between white and black, male and female, and so forth. One way of solving the sexual bipolarity was to make everyone female, including Dicky—or everyone male, including herself. She was preoccupied with color because she was using the fact that she was Negro to explain her failures, just as many people ascribe their misfortunes to being a woman, not going to college, or some other fact of life.

Depression and Hostility

The caseworker became increasingly concerned about Mrs. T's continued depression and her overt hostility. The worker was afraid that she might have become involved in the client's paranoid system, in which she would eventually become the focus of all the hostility. What the caseworker did not recognize was that Mrs. T's manifestations were not paranoid but were characteristic responses of persons with character disorders in the third stage of treatment. Mrs. T's depressions at this time were probably neither more severe nor more frequent than they had been previously, but they were more apparent. The reasons were twofold: (1) Mrs. T was now comfortable enough with the caseworker to reveal her actual feelings, and (2) since Mrs. T no longer used acting out as a defense against depression, she now felt the depression as such. In order to work through the depression, Mrs. T had need to lean on a strong person, one whom she considered omnipotent. She therefore invested the caseworker with tremendous power to give and to withhold in relation to all her wishes. To be placed in this kind of omnipotent

129

role and to be the object of the aggression that accompanies it can be extremely frightening.

For a time, Mrs. T's concentration on the caseworker was partially deflected. She joined a weight-control group, led by a psychiatrist. Her decision to join was precipitated by two events: a physician whom she had consulted alarmed her about her obesity, and she had a blowup with Dicky, who was 10 at the time. Mrs. T's report of the incident is recorded as follows:

On Tuesday, Mrs. T and Dicky got into a fight over his homework. She told him that if he wanted to be only a dishwasher, he could stay home and wash her dishes. After Mrs. T's temper subsided, they had talked for three hours. Dicky said he had ambitions and wanted to be something, but he was not going to be forced. He said he could do arithmetic, but he wasn't trying. He knew it was no use to fight with his mother, but he could spite her by not doing his work. He said she called him a "bushman," but he said she was a "bushwoman" herself. He added that the trouble with Mrs. T was that she had no confidence in herself, that she could write and do lots of things but she didn't do them. He said she got upset about Dicky's being friends with Negro children, but didn't she know that you could be nice to people without being their best friends? He had given up taking two Negro boys to the club because he recognized that they didn't fit in. The other kids said, "We're glad you left your brats at home."

He said he had started his homework strike against his mother to make her mad, but he didn't mean to break up the home. He then brought out his worry about the adoption, saying, "If your own mother can give you away, how do you know your adopted mother won't do the same thing?" He asked why his mother gave him up. Was there something wrong with him? He wanted to see his birth certificate and Mrs. T promised to get a copy for him.

Mrs. T told me that she was struck by the things he said about her pushing him, by his fear of losing her, and so forth, since these were the same things the caseworker had said several times. In the end, she and Dicky made a pact; he was to do his arithmetic and she was to reduce. She had never realized that he was ashamed of her. He said her coat made her look like a "Pilgrim mother." This last remark was obviously an expression of his fear of her becoming pregnant, which was then discussed. Mrs. T was very pleased by his ability to "talk up" to her. She could not stand submission. She spoke of his telling more to her than

130

to his caseworker. I said it was good for him to speak frankly to her because she was his mother. She then gave Mr. F credit for helping Dicky and wanted me to be sure to tell him about this incident. She also decided to accept money from the agency for Dicky's camp.

Mrs. T's experience in the weight-control group was a tremendous success. Contrary to her former pattern, she did not take on the leader as a parent but constituted herself an assistant leader. At first she pretended to herself that she was the caseworker and later was not sure what role she was playing. She lost more weight than anyone else, and she became friendly on an equal basis with a white college woman who had begun by offering her a job as a maid. She had handled the incident with poise and dignity.

In the spring, as a result of her identification with a young Negro counselor, she undertook to cook for the boys' club annual camping expedition. During one afternoon when the group was left in the charge of inept junior counselors, a mutiny developed. She thought to herself, "What is the democratic way of handling this?" and then said, "In a democracy, if you don't like your officials, you impeach them." So she got the boys busy organizing a court.

After her period at the camp, her old depression returned, together with anger against the caseworker, to whom she attributed a wish to control her. She also was angry at Dicky, commenting, "He's not my kind of child." Suddenly, as she said this, she realized that as a child she had been as lazy as he, since both her mother and her grandmother had pampered her. They had intended her to be an intellectual who would never do menial work. Her clothes had always been in the latest style. Then her mother died and everything changed. She recalled that she had gradually learned to work but that it had not been easy.

Mrs. T then took a summer job in the kitchen of a girl's camp, although she had some misgivings about how she would get along with the other Negro personnel. She obviously had a need to swing between being hyperactive and being depressed. The swing represented the two possible roles between which she had to choose and both of which she wanted—the active, independent male role and the passive, dependent female role. Mrs. T's wish for the female role at this time was demonstrated by increased references in her conversation to the women in her family and by electing to work in a girl's camp.

She returned in the fall, proud that there had been no blowups and that she had recognized the chief cook's attachment to the woman director and had refrained from interfering. She was upset and depressed, however, by the fact that the cook knew Mrs. T's maternal relatives and praised them excessively. Mrs. T had always been angry because none of them had been willing to take her after her grandmother's death and that they had allowed her to live haphazardly, and finally be placed by an agency. She had reacted to the cook's praise of this family by saying she was her father's daughter. However, she remembered her father as a "bad" and frightening person. This remark reveals that Mrs. T's anal quality was at work again. She had to balance the situation by comparing her father with her maternal relatives—male versus female, bad versus good.

This discussion of her past reactivated Mrs. T's depression. It was further increased by uncertainty about cooking classes, by Dicky's sudden refusal to visit their old neighborhood (where people had made references to his real mother), and by the news that their block was to be demolished to make room for a housing project. In addition, the public welfare worker was placing pressure on Mrs. T to get a job. Her reaction to the pressure was passive resistance in the form of talking about "plans" which were quite nebulous.

At one point, Mrs. T telephoned the caseworker to announce, with a kind of chilling, withdrawn hostility, that she had sent Dicky to the agency for placement, since she was going away. The caseworker handled the crisis by making a home visit. She expressed concern about Mrs. T, making it clear that no one would take the maternal role away from Mrs. T. This point was expressed concretely by stating that the agency had neither the wish nor the right to place Dicky. Before the caseworker left, Mrs. T appeared to feel better. In this episode she was acting out the loss of her mother by threatening to make Dicky lose his, and utilizing the mechanism of identification with the aggressor.

Soon after this incident, Mrs. T was admitted to the cooking school as a special adult student. However, her depression continued. She complained that the school was like a reformatory and

132

she was ambivalent toward the mother substitutes she found there. She regressed to the level of her teen-age companions and competed with them for special privileges.

Her dissatisfaction with Dicky also continued and it finally became clear that she was interpreting his sensitivity about being adopted as rejection of her. When it was clarified that, on the contrary, he was afraid of losing her, she seemed relieved. A discussion of the fantasy that adopted children often have about their mothers and about the mysterious quality called "mother love" seemed also to be relieving. Mrs. T complained about Dicky's not spending more time with her and she continued to urge that her caseworker, rather than Mr. F, see Dicky. She confessed that she had been jealous of Dicky, afraid that he "came first" with the caseworker. She then commented that he was "mine and yours" and that no one else should "get into this." Dicky, now 11, was developing an unrealistic idea of going to Latin school and ultimately becoming a social worker, obviously in an attempt to be like the club counselor whom his mother admired. He was also responding to her wish for a mother; by becoming a social worker, he could play this role for her. His educational aim represented a desperate attempt to meet her needs. Mrs. T recognized the lack of reality in his plan and was annoyed by it. She said that if he were really her child, he would be able to carry it through and she would make any sacrifice to help him.

One night Mrs. T had a dream that frightened her. She dreamed that her grandfather wrote to her, stating she was the only one left and that her father wanted to see her. She said she never remembered dreams, except for one the week before her mother died, so she believed this dream was an ominous sign. In the childhood dream she was in heaven looking down on her mother's funeral. The caseworker asked how much she had been aware of what was happening to her mother at the time of her death. She said she had known that something was wrong, but not that her mother was pregnant. She had been anxious about her mother's getting fat but she had thought it was from eating oatmeal. She had opened a drawer and found it full of baby clothes. She had been overjoyed, thinking they were doll clothes for her for Christmas. This memory contained the chief source of her depression—the disillusionment about her mother's providing for her needs and, immediately following this, the loss of the mother. She had been looking for a mother and had found only a dead one.

Mrs. T now reported that the building she lived in would be torn down in three or four months and that she was doing nothing about looking for another place to live. She said she was tired because she had not had a vacation last summer. The caseworker said Mrs. T had been upset last summer by being reminded of her family and that the dream about her father might be connected with this upset. Mrs. T recalled that, during the previous summer, she had felt that she was like her father and that she did not blame him for breaking up the home. She said, however, that she could remember his fighting with her mother and that she and her mother had sometimes hidden under the bed. Mrs. T mentioned that she had always called her mother "Mabel" and that she was more upset by her grandmother's death than by her mother's. Mrs. T then said she liked to tell the caseworker things because the latter seemed to feel as bad as she did, and then she felt better.

The Relationship

Mrs. T's comment suggests that, even if one does not know the full significance in dynamic terms of what the client is saying, the caseworker's empathy has certain therapeutic value. This is especially true in the third stage of treatment, when it is important for the client to sense that his feelings are understood and accepted. Such acceptance reassures him that his hostility is not reciprocated and supports him in his efforts to grow up and act independently. If the caseworker does not recognize the source of both the depression and the hostility, he will react negatively in spite of himself and, as a result, this period of treatment will be prolonged. The client's excessive search for a love object, which also threatens to engulf the caseworker, may be even more frightening than the hostility. In the client's swing of emotion, the caseworker may make the error of choosing to emphasize the hostility because it seems safer.

The threatened loss of shelter reinforced Mrs. T's sense of homelessness and heightened her preoccupation with the question of "Who is at fault?" She was confronted with her feelings of loss and the fear of the self (the building) collapsing. Her memory about the wish for the doll clothes suggests that she felt that wishing to have things for herself might lead to the loss of everything. This fear provides a clue to the magical meaning of Mrs. T's extreme renunciation of clothes, furniture, and so forth. The material she presented also suggests that, when her mother died, she did not face the total impact of the loss since she still had her grandmother. Her relationship to her mother was partially that of sibling and of a competitor for mothering from the grandmother. As a result, she doubtless had excessive hostility toward the mother and compensatory overidealization after her death.

An episode occurred at this time whose meaning was not clear to the caseworker until later. Mrs. T had begun to think that she might consider applying to a housing project, in spite of her earlier objections. She reported by telephone that she had gone to inspect one and had dropped in to see a former family agency supervisor, who now worked in an office near that project. The caseworker remarked on the telephone that this would be a convenient office for Mrs. T to use. When Mrs. T came for her appointment, she was in a fury at the housing authority, saying that she could never stand being under their control. She said she would not move to a project, even if the only alternative was to live with Dicky in one furnished room "under the bridge." By "under the bridge," she meant a rooming-house neighborhood beyond the railroad bridge near the worker's office. The caseworker recognized that Mrs. T was making a threat, since the worker had often talked about the need for privacy for both Mrs. T and Dicky. Subsequently, the reason for Mrs. T's hostile outbursts became evident. She revealed that she thought that, if she moved to a project, she would be transferred to another agency office. Mrs. T evidently had sensed the caseworker's countertransference reaction at the time of the telephone conversation. The caseworker had thought Mrs. T might be transferred to the other office; she had felt some relief and, at the same time, some resentment that Mrs. T, who had recently been showing so much hostility, would prefer a change. The caseworker had reacted like a parent who does not recognize the child's fear of rejection which accompanies his struggle for independence and who therefore is hurt by his continuous hostility. After the caseworker understood Mrs. T's fear of losing the relationship, she offered to continue to see Mrs. T as long as she needed help. After this, Mrs. T, reassured that she could be independent and still continue the relationship, gave up much of her regressive acting out.

Improvement in Functioning

Mrs. T ended the third stage of treatment with a flurry of activity. She abandoned her campaign to be accepted as a regular pupil at the trade school and announced to the caseworker that she was finished with high school and ready to take a job. She said she now wanted to be a woman and to give up being a baby. The caseworker accepted this new role by providing her with a coat she needed, thinking that if Mrs. T was to face the world as a woman she should be dressed like one. Mrs. T moved into a housing project which, to her surprise, she liked. She responded to an act of control by the public assistance worker not with a tantrum but with an active hunt for a job. Her first job was cooking in a restaurant where she was under much pressure. She gave this up after a week and took the first thing available, which was a factory job. She has remained there for the past five years.

After Mrs. T moved to the new apartment, important changes took place in her relationship with Dicky. One morning after an argument, he went out saying, "Don't cook any supper for me; I'm going to my own people." When he returned he asked where his supper was. Mrs. T said, "I thought you were going to your own people." He said, "I changed my mind." She said, "It's a good thing you did because you haven't any people—I'm your people." He sat down as if stunned. In spite of Mrs. T's previous explanations, he had thought that adoption was a kind of temporary custody and that eventually his own people would claim him. Mrs. T's ability now to convey to him that she was his mother was part of her growth to womanhood; he responded with obvious relief.

After Mrs. T had worked a few weeks in the factory, she invited the caseworker to visit her at the housing project. She seemed quite self-assured and capable in managing her home and her affairs. The caseworker offered help toward Dicky's camp fee as a loan rather than as an outright gift, as a recognition of the change in Mrs. T. Formerly help had always been extended as a gift.

During this visit, Mrs. T asked advice about Blue Cross membership, saying that she would need it when she had a baby. The caseworker calmly agreed that in that case she would need the more expensive group plan. Mrs. T then indicated that she was troubled about this wish for a baby, which seemed in so many ways so irrational, and also about her unreasonable anger whenever she found a Negro occupying an important position. The caseworker offered to try to help her understand these two feelings which seemed to cause her difficulty. It was tacitly agreed that Mrs. T was asking for continued help.

Appraisal

In the case of Mrs. T, the third stage of treatment covered thirty months. Undoubtedly this time could have been shortened if the caseworker at various points had been more fully aware of the meaning of Mrs. T's behavior. For instance, it probably was unnecessary for Mrs. T to relive her adolescence so literally as she did in the school experience. With help from the caseworker in seeing the irrationality of her demand for equal status with high school sophomores, she might have been able to live through it symbolically, and therefore more quickly. Also, if the caseworker had recognized that Mrs. T's increased depression and hostility were signs of her need to achieve independence and to test out her new identity, the contact would have been smoother. Not understanding the dynamics fully, the caseworker had to struggle with her own countertransference feelings—her fear of being involved in a paranoid psychotic system and her alternating anxiety and anger in response to Mrs. T's intensified emotional attitudes.

The fact that the case continued in spite of these hazards can be attributed to the perseverance of both the client and the caseworker. The client, who was basically a bright and intuitive woman, had a strong perception that she had found someone who could help her. Another factor that favored treatment was her tenacity. It was the tenacity of the oral character toward any love object and the stubbornness of the anal-erotic character in handling life situations. The caseworker, on her part, not only recognized the client's potential for growth but she did not give up easily, holding the belief that a ship can be steered so long as it is in motion.

Gains in Third Stage of Treatment

The third stage of treatment is marked by the client's struggle to achieve emotional separation from the caseworker and an identity of his own. As indicated earlier, the struggle corresponds closely to the effort of the adolescent child to free himself from his parents. Such effort often can be made by clients with character disorders if they have first experienced a period of dependence on the caseworker during which they work through some of their infantile modes of behavior and develop some ego strength. If pregenital problems are sufficiently worked through, the residuals of the early traumas will be expressed more in neurotic ways and less in acting-out behavior. At this point, it is possible for these clients to sublimate some of their pregenital impulses and to achieve some reorganization of their character structures.

The techniques of the third stage of treatment have special application to clients whose character traits are related to the phallic-urethral stage of psychosexual development, since these clients are already searching for identity. Often, treatment may actually begin with efforts to develop their independence and to help them accept their masculinity or femininity. They have less need to use the caseworker as a source for primitive mothering than do persons fixated at oral and anal levels. They are better able, from the outset, to use the caseworker as a model.

In the case of Mrs. Stowe, the caseworker from the beginning directed the relationship toward helping Mrs. S be more feminine and to have less mistrust of her feelings which she regarded as female and, therefore, weak. The techniques involved discussion of external manifestations of femininity, such as hairdos and clothes, as well as internal conflicts. She was helped to see the obvious contradiction between her perception of her feelings and her verbal denial of them. This approach differs somewhat from the techniques used with clients who have anal characters and are not conscious of their feelings. In treatment, the technique was not one of training her to be more aware of these feelings, but rather of helping her to use them. For instance, Mrs. S had to learn to tell her son, Ralph, when she left the house, that she would soon return. She recognized that he was fearful, but she had treated his fears as she did her own, that is, by ignoring them because she thought they were childish. In the same way, it was possible to help her work through some of her own problems about sexual identity by discussing problems she recognized in her adolescent son, Robert.

One of the problems in the contact with adult clients who are seeking to develop an identity is the emergence of homosexual strivings directed toward the therapist. These feelings can be a source of discomfort to both client and caseworker. The caseworker may become alarmed and guilty if he fails to recognize the phenomenon as part of the client's struggle for identity. He may be uneasy about how to respond to the client's libidinal overtures, and feel guilty because he fears he somehow stimulated them. If the overtures are recognized as part of a testing-out process that is similar to adolescent behavior, the caseworker should be able to respond appropriately, neither rebuffing the client nor reciprocating the emotion. What the client needs at this point is a strong parental figure who can understand and appreciate his struggle to grow up and become a man or a woman. It is important for the therapist to have established satisfactorily his own sexual identification.

In certain cases, where there is evidence of ego development sufficient for repression, the question arises about how to combine experiential techniques that are appropriate for the treatment of clients with character disorders with uncovering techniques. Obviously, when neurotic symptoms are present, attempts should be made to involve the client in focused discussion of these problems, but they should be timed in relation to his capacity to work on them.

This question is similar to the one that arises at the end of the third stage of treatment of a character disorder. It is sometimes difficult to know whether the client will be able to use a therapeutic approach that is different from the one to which he is accustomed. Two criteria for undertaking treatment utilizing uncovering techniques are: evidence that the client has developed a fairly strong sense of identity and that he has manifested ability to act with independence and judgment, rather than in an impulsive way. He should also have developed a relatively well-integrated concept of sexuality and should be displaying his conflicts through symptoms rather than through acting-out behavior.

139

VIII. The Fourth Stage of Treatment:
Helping the Client Gain Self-understanding

DURING THE FOURTH STAGE of treatment the caseworker's aim is to help the client gain some understanding of his behavior and its roots in the past. This phase of treatment can be initiated with the client who has a character disorder only after he has worked through his preoedipal fixations with relative success. At this point he has experienced a long period of identification with the caseworker which has provided opportunity for him to incorporate new concepts and values. He has lived through various steps in the maturing process which have culminated in sufficient resolution of his infantile equivalent of a transference neurosis to enable him to make an emotional separation from the caseworker and to establish his own identity.

The separation does not require renunciation of the relationship any more than liberation from the parents in adolescence requires complete severance of parental ties. The successful solution of adolescent problems means that the child, having achieved an identity of his own, is capable of a different kind of parental relationship. He can still accept help and guidance when it is appropriate but he does so on a more mature level.

It is important for the caseworker to understand that the client, like an adolescent, may have changed sufficiently to engage in a mature relationship. The changes are observable both in the client's relationship to the worker and in the content of his discussions. Three indications of such changes are: (1) The client is able to take independent action and to make mature decisions, that is, decisions based on realistic factors. (2) The client's requests for help imply that he expects to participate in working on his problems and to take responsibility for finding solutions for them. (3) The content of the material he presents is more oedipal in nature, that is, it involves triangular situations or symbolism.

Further Analysis of the Tenney Case

The three responses listed above were evident in Mrs. Tenney at the time the caseworker offered to help her gain some understanding about her preoccupation with her wish to have a baby and her feeling about Negroes. Up to this point, casework had been focused on helping Mrs. T work through her underlying depression. She now seemed able to deal with some of her oedipal problems, much as a neurotic would. Prior to this time, she had often insisted that the caseworker could, if she would, help her with these problems, and that it was unnecessary to send her to a psychiatrist. Although she had verbalized her wish for such help, she had made treatment of the oedipal problems impossible by the constant acting out of her dependency.

As indicated in the preceding chapter, it was agreed that Mrs. T would now begin work on these problems, even though she said it upset her to talk about these feelings. She objected to the caseworker's comment that Mrs. T thought that being a Negro meant that one was inferior. She struggled to express her feeling of not belonging anywhere and spoke of her wish to care for "lost Negro children." On one level, the wish was her own wish to be found and cared for; she was the lost Negro child. On another level, the wish expressed a desire for a more sublimated solution—to be a parent because of her new identification with a parent figure. Her attitude about religion was indicative of her feelings about being "lost." She said that when things were going well, she felt that God loved her, but when she was angry and depressed she felt that even God had deserted her. It was clear that the deeper reason for her feeling of not belonging anywhere was not her dark skin but the infantile "dirty," incestuous part of herself with which her dark skin was equated in her mind.

141

The material she discussed was not new; the themes had recurred frequently, throughout the entire period of treatment. Although listening to such repetitive reports may be tiresome to the caseworker, he should keep in mind that the client develops the themes in different ways at different stages of treatment and that the variations represent different levels of the personality.

The Wish for a Baby

Mrs. T's recurrent wish for a baby had several meanings. At times, the baby represented her wish to have someone to love and through whom she could enjoy vicariously the experience of being mothered. At other times, it represented an act of defiance against a hostile world that disregarded her needs. In addition, Mrs. T perceived the baby as an "incestuous" one, fathered by her white friend George or some other paternal figure. Another meaning, which was perhaps paramount at this time, was her own rebirth; her fantasy now was that the baby would be a girl and one who would not be hurt by the vicissitudes of life. The caseworker understood Mrs. T to mean "in contrast to Dicky," who had had such a hard time and had caused her so much trouble, but, on a deeper level, she doubtless meant in contrast to herself. All these meanings had to be explored and discussed, at least in part, before the urgency of the wish could be dissipated. In other words, it was important to remember that a fantasy or symptom is "multiply determined" and that its various determinants must be examined.

When the caseworker began to confront Mrs. T with her wish for an incestuous baby, she became angry and for a time she blocked on the subject. Later she brought in magazine articles on marriage, endeavoring to prove that women are controlled and pushed down while men get the best of everything. She said she mistrusted men. She added that, to her, love was not tied to sex. Sex was like whiskey—she could take it or leave it alone. She said she had been in love only once, and that was with George (the white lawyer). She also said she could get along with a man for a while and then forget him, but she sounded as if she was not sure that this was really true.

In these comments, Mrs. T was bringing up the question that an adolescent girl asks: Does the man use the woman sexually and

142

then leave her? In the broadest sense the question is: What do I lose by giving in to sexual and aggressive feelings? Mrs. T obviously was curious about sex and also afraid of it. We might expect her to swing back and forth between sexual feelings and her fear of losing her mother, since she had reached the stage of adolescent conflict. The question, "Why doesn't my mother love me?" is a frightening one. Its answer in the unconscious is, "Because I want to kill her, because I want relations with my father, and because I have dirty thoughts."

The material Mrs. T presented was clearly oedipal in nature, with the triadic situation of mother, father, and child. Her relationship with George obviously combined both the wish for a mother and for a man. Mrs. T's current wish for a mother was not, as formerly, for an all-gratifying one but for one who would protect her against her incestuous wishes, and with whom she could identify as a woman; this identification would enable her to have satisfactory outlets for feelings which up to now had caused only trouble. She talked enviously of an adolescent girl who was illegitimately pregnant and who planned to keep the baby, not caring what anyone thought. Mrs. T said, however, that she did care what the caseworker thought. She said this ambivalently, as if the caseworker represented both a handicap and a protection.

She obviously was frightened of her incestuous wishes and kept asking for protection against them. She said that she always got what she really wanted and that she knew this was dangerous. In this connection, she told of her competitive need to be the best, both in the factory where she worked and, earlier, as a child in school. It was evident in her report of her competition that penis symbolism was associated with it, and that she equated being the "best" with masculinity. Having a baby, too, was associated with having a penis. Her incestuous wishes and her envy of masculinity were accompanied by the kind of omnipotent fantasies typical of the phallic-urethral stage of development. These fantasies are characterized by a sense of grandiosity, power, and ability to control, and are expressed in exhibitionism and pride. While Mrs. T was challenging the caseworker to help her get rid of the fantasy of having a baby, she acted as if the fantasy were real, by collecting baby foods for the postnatal period and by taking a course in power-machine operating to earn "big money" to support the baby. She referred to herself as "split," quoting a newspaper article by a man who had been mentally ill and whose fantasies were "realer than reality." She said that the picture of the baby was sharp and clear in her mind, but part of her knew it was not sensible to have one— that was why she was asking for help.

Like the adolescent who speaks of himself as "crazy," Mrs. T was aware of the impulses that were pulling her back to pregenital fantasies. At this stage of treatment, it is particularly important not to accept the fantasies literally, but to support their ego-alien quality and thus enable the client to use fantasy rather than behavior as the outlet. In order to achieve this goal, the caseworker should convey the idea that the client can deal with reality; the worker need not discuss the fantasy, but he can provide support by letting the client know he is not afraid that the client will act out the fantasy.

In this instance, the caseworker provided such support by continuing to explore with Mrs. T the pregnancy material she had brought up. Mrs. T said she had no right to have an illegitimate baby since the agency had been so good to her. The caseworker said that evidently having a baby meant to her an act of defiance (or feeling unloved). Mrs. T then talked about the refusal of her maternal relatives to take her in during her adolescence because they had heard that she was wild and difficult to manage. Later she revealed more about her identification with the standards of her white, maternal grandmother and her own rebellion against them. She also made it clear that she had begun to lose her grandmother at the time of her mother's death. Not only did her grandmother become depressed and withdrawn, but she worked long hours and usually came home tired. It seems apparent that Mrs. T must have felt at the time that she lost the people she loved because of her "bad" thoughts and wishes.

Questions about Femininity

Mrs. T also gave information that explained some of her feelings about men. Until the age of six she was loved and made much of by her maternal grandfather, which helped to counteract some of her fear of her father. His affection doubtless set up an oedipal situation for Mrs. T in relation to the grandmother. The oedipal situation was re-enacted traumatically for Mrs. T when, some time after her grandfather's death, she went on the honeymoon with her mother and stepfather. On the honeymoon she slept in another bed in the same room (the fantasy of "Frankie" in *Member of the Wedding*). After her grandmother's death she turned to her stepfather for mothering, which was accompanied by sexual fantasy if not sexual activity. It would seem that her relationship with George was a re-enactment of the relationship with the stepfather.

In the interviews, Mrs. T referred to the publicity about Christine Jorgensen (a man who became a woman through surgery). She used the story to explain her concern about her genitals; she finally made it clear that she had an extra piece of flesh which seemed to her like a residual penis. She accepted referral to a gynecologist who reported that one of the labia was longer than the other. It seems likely that Mrs. T was able to go through a gynecological examination at this time because she now wished to be a woman and to get rid of the male part of herself which was causing trouble. It is common for people to hope to find some surgical or medical means of treatment for whatever they think is not right with them. It is also common for women to avoid physical examination—as Mrs. T had done earlier—in order to continue the bisexual fantasy.

Curiously, at the same time that Mrs. T was attempting to get rid of the male part of herself, she had taken a man's job running a heavy machine in the factory. It paid relatively high wages and enabled her to work alone at her own rate of speed and be on an equal basis with the men. However, she was taking more pleasure in feminine tasks at home and had begun to revive her former interest in art which had been encouraged by one foster mother and by George. Thus, in her occupational activities she was sublimating her struggle about body identity.

In this connection it should be noted that sublimation is a way of dealing with unresolved pregenital struggles and that it cannot take place until the individual has worked out some of the fantasies associated with the original pregenital strivings.[1] In other words, there must be a decathexis at the pregenital level of the

---

[1] Otto Fenichel, M.D., *The Psychoanalytical Theory of Neurosis*, W. W. Norton and Co., New York, 1945, p. 141.

original libidinal and aggressive investment so that this energy can be freed and invested in environmental activities; for example, the wish to smear is sublimated into the wish to paint. Caseworkers tend to hope that the client can successfully utilize his psychic energy in dealing with the environment at a premature stage, that is, before the underlying conflict has been resolved and before the necessary decathexis has taken place. This understanding is of utmost importance for "manipulative casework."[2]

Discussion of the results of the gynecological examination revealed clearly Mrs. T's wish to be a woman rather than a "half person," as she put it. A discussion of the anatomical facts led directly to the subjects of masturbation and homosexuality, which were connected in her mind. Mrs. T did not reveal this confusion until after she had reviewed her relationship with George. In the earlier interviews, Mrs. T had given several brief and sketchy versions of this affair, but the caseworker had not encouraged her to go into it fully, since Mrs. T had no motivation for trying to understand it. This time she told the whole story, including the fact that she had really seduced George and that she had been frightened when he responded sexually. Throughout the six or seven years of their clandestine affair she had lived in fear of what might happen to George professionally if their relationship became known. After he had been elected to political office, Mrs. T realized that there was no future in the relationship for her and that it was too dangerous for him. She did not make clear whether there was actual rejection on his part or merely a turning away from her. She then began to seek more contacts with the Negro group. She became intimate with Richard, whom she married soon thereafter. His mother had died recently and he obviously was searching for someone to mother him. He continued his search after marriage, having affairs with many girls; Mrs. T said she had not really been angry with him at the time because she felt that she was failing him. She was still preoccupied with fantasies concerning George and in her fantasy Dicky became George's baby rather than Richard's. Later, she began to see Richard's characteristics in Dicky and to be angry because he was not like George.

[2] Grete L. Bibring, M.D., "Psychiatric Principles in Casework," *Journal of Social Casework*, Vol. XXX, No. 6 (1949), pp. 230–231.

In discussing Mrs. T's relationship with George, the caseworker emphasized first that Mrs. T had been attracted to him because of her need for a family and for love, pointing out that Mrs. T had been loved before and desperately wanted to be loved again. This explanation led Mrs. T to talk about her loneliness and anger during her placements in childhood and to describe her defensive acting-out behavior at that time. After this discussion, the caseworker encouraged Mrs. T to talk about the reality aspects of her relationship with George, that is, the actual things they had done and enjoyed together. There was considerable evidence that the relationship had had depth and meaning for both of them. Finally, Mrs. T spoke of her unhappiness in not being able to show her grief openly at his funeral. She told of her recent envy of a politician's widow, who could cry and receive sympathy at her husband's funeral. When Mrs. T seemed to have reached the end of the subject she expressed considerable relief, saying that other people to whom she had talked about George had taken the attitude that he was an ogre.

Her relief indicated that some of her guilt had been allayed. The reduction of guilt seems to have been brought about chiefly in two ways: (1) the caseworker did not minimize Mrs. T's part in the seduction of George, and (2) she acknowledged the importance of the relationship both to Mrs. T and to George. In addition, the discussion of the reality aspects of the experience took it out of the realm of fantasy and made it a real part of Mrs. T's past. Such reduction of fantasy elements was possible because she had already partially worked out her fantasy wish for a mother.

Sexual Conflicts

Mrs. T then mentioned her fear that the sexual relations with George had caused her genital malformation. This fear of her aggression, projected onto George in the ogre concept, represented both her guilt about her seduction of George and her belief that women are hurt by men. On a deeper level (related to her wish to become male) she may have felt that she had taken his penis; her wish to possess it may have been equated with her wish to hold on to parental figures. Her sexual relationship with George was partly an altruistic surrender, motivated by her guilt about her

147

primitive wish to take his penis. Her admitted lack of interest in sexual relations may have been due to frigidity—an anesthesia that serves as a denial of the primitive wish to castrate or destroy and to protect and preserve the needed love object.

In subsequent interviews, Mrs. T spoke of her guilt about masturbation and her fear of homosexuality. To her, masturbation meant turning against men. She associated it with her fantasies about George, saying she thought about him when she felt depressed, deserted, and unloved. It was clear that Mrs. T dealt with feelings of loss by some sexual process; in masturbation she directed her libido both toward persons and toward self. However, when persons deserted her, she turned toward herself both the libido and the anger about the desertion. Therefore, the turning toward the self included an attack upon herself. She felt that she was deserted because she was no good. In the treatment of Mrs. T, it was important to help her understand this process. An attempt merely to relieve her guilt about masturbation would not have been effective since it would not have helped her understand the struggle that precipitated the masturbation. It was necessary to help Mrs. T see that when she turned away from external love objects she used masturbation as a way both to attack herself and to deal with her anxiety and depression.

In referring to her contacts with women, Mrs. T said that people had questioned her relationship with Miss Brooks but not with the former district supervisor or the present caseworker, and yet the difference was only in intensity. Mrs. T stated that Miss Brooks had stirred up deep feelings in her because Miss Brooks resembled George and had responded to her in a more personal way than the present caseworker. Mrs. T said that she had been smarter in limiting the relationship with the latter, adding, "I had to because you did." She said that the present worker helped her in this respect because she did not let Mrs. T control her. Mrs. T knew, however, that the worker liked her.

She continued to talk about her homosexual tendencies and on one occasion brought in a love poem she had written with Miss Brooks in mind which people always assumed was addressed to a man. The caseworker said it expressed a kind of universal feeling of love; this comment seemed acceptable to Mrs. T. The caseworker then spoke of Mrs. T's mixed feelings about women as well as of the fact that she had received considerable love from her mother and grandmother even though they had disappointed her in many ways. The worker said that most girls are able to grow up and move into relationships with men because they have a close relationship with a mother or girl friend who helps them in this direction. Mrs. T said, "My life is all mixed up. I have done things backwards. I have done them first and I am just learning about them now. Maybe I am beginning to grow up."

The material Mrs. T presented about her homosexual interests illustrates her effort to work out the old oedipal struggle. It is obvious that she was swinging back and forth between her identity as a man and as a woman, and that she needed help in establishing her identification as a woman. Little would have been gained by a theoretical discussion of social or cultural aspects of homosexuality.

It suddenly seemed to dawn on Mrs. T that she had been thinking less about having a baby. She stated that she had begun to think less about it after the caseworker had suggested, about three months earlier, that Mrs. T might like to serve as a foster mother. The worker had told her that a child-placing agency had advertised for women who would give temporary care to undernourished babies. Mrs. T had been delighted with the idea, saying that she would love to care for a baby and see him improve, but had no need to hang on to a child. It seems likely that Mrs. T interpreted the caseworker's suggestion as permission for her to have a baby in a legitimate way and, as a result, her need to hold on to the fantasy of giving birth to one was lessened. Earlier, Mrs. T had shown obvious relief when the worker had pointed out (in connection with the discussion of masturbation) that a baby was someone whom it was safe to love and that, in fantasy, Mrs. T herself was the baby who would get some of the desired love. The end of Mrs. T's fantasy about having an illegitimate baby became evident to Mrs. T when she canceled the medical plan covering maternity care.

Throughout the period when Mrs. T was discussing her wish to have a baby, the caseworker had to consider how best to respond to her. Even when one recognizes that such a wish is a fantasy, one is fearful that the client may act out the fantasy. Although acting out is always a possibility, the caseworker's best chance of helping

149

the client is to endeavor to reduce the fantasy. As with any fantasy, it is the meaning that is important. The meaning may not be apparent initially either to client or to caseworker, but the process of endeavoring to understand its sources can have therapeutic value to the client. Mrs. T's almost automatic cancellation of the medical-care plan illustrates how emotional decisions are made. Too often caseworkers expect such decisions to be made intellectually or as an act of will.

Mrs. T soon began to talk more about Dicky and his adolescent problems. She seemed genuinely concerned about making realistic plans for the future of both Dicky and herself. Discussion of Dicky's adolescent struggles gave opportunity to help Mrs. T work out her own residual problems stemming from the same level of development. Fortunately, Dicky's early adolescence coincided with this stage of Mrs. T's therapy.

Termination of Contact

Although Mrs. T continued to hold a man's job, she reduced her hours of work so that she would have more time at home to do a woman's work. She commented at this time that she now had a feeling that most things would work out in some way and that she did not need to know in advance exactly how. Now that she had largely worked out her identification problems, she did not need to hold various alternatives before her all of the time. She therefore had more energy to deal with the current reality. She reported Dicky's sayings and doings with a new pleasure. She said he need not necessarily be bright in order to please her. She recognized that her wish for him to be a social worker had been only an extension of the same wish for herself. Now that she could be herself, she could allow Dicky to be himself.

In response to a mild suggestion that Mrs. T no longer needed the caseworker's help, Mrs. T began to taper off the contact. Actually, she terminated the contact herself. In one of her last sessions, she talked about a book called *The Gentle House*, which is about a boy who had come to this country as a displaced person. He reminded her of herself since he, too, had been difficult to get along with. She said the reason the caseworker had been able to

150

help her was that she never got angry with Mrs. T. The caseworker then told her that she was leaving the agency but explained where she could be reached. She added that she would always be interested in knowing how Mrs. T was getting along. Mrs. T then confessed that she knew the caseworker's home address and expressed pride that she had never made use of it.

Follow-up Reports

For four years after termination of contact, the caseworker received occasional communications from Mrs. T. She continued to work at the same job and received several sizable pay increases. She pursued her study of art, although she resisted her teacher's attempts to push her into exhibiting. There was evidence that she still was depressed at times. She continued to be overweight and her social life was somewhat limited. These problems, however, trouble a large number of relatively adequate people. Her adaptation was quite different from that of her earlier years, when her severe character disturbance left her almost completely at the mercy of her primitive impulses.

Dicky had some of the usual adolescent problems, expressed largely in poor school attendance. His truancy decreased after he transferred to a trade school. Also, membership in a settlement house group was a stabilizing force for him. Mrs. T appeared to have handled the various situations that arose quite well. She seemed willing for Dicky to have girl friends.

One day, four years after the case had been closed, Mrs. T telephoned the caseworker, saying that she wanted to thank her for something. She said she first would have to explain what she meant by telling a story. One night, not long before, there had been a knock at the door and when she opened it she was startled to see a man with a face very like her own. He turned out to be her younger half-brother whom she had not seen for years. In the course of their conversation, he invited her to come to visit him and his new wife. They also talked a little about themselves and he said he always had been looking for something. He thought he had now found it in his marriage.

Mrs. T put off the visit for some time. When she did go, she was favorably impressed by the wife and the apartment. After a time, her brother interrupted the pleasant conversation by demanding ten dollars from his wife. When she asked why he wanted it, he went into a rage, throwing things and breaking the furniture. Mrs. T had sat watching him quietly, thinking to herself that he acted the way she formerly did. All she could think of was how much she had changed. She wondered how the caseworker had put up with her and she wanted to thank her.

Gains in Fourth Stage of Treatment

This phase of the case of Mrs. T serves to illustrate the difference in techniques used in therapy after a client with a character disorder has reached the oedipal stage. As indicated earlier, the content of the material may not be appreciably different, but the client's purpose in telling it is different. Also emphasis on certain experiences is heightened and the emotions attached to them are more frankly expressed. The client no longer uses personal history as a rationalization for his difficulties or as part of the amorphous verbalization that had accompanied his earlier acting out of pregenital problems. In a mature way, he now tries to understand what has happened to him and, through such understanding, to overcome his particular limitations. He approaches the task as an adult and not as an infant seeking to be fed or as a child struggling with the training process or wavering between the wish and fear of becoming a man or woman. In this stage of treatment, the caseworker does not primarily need to demonstrate the parental role by offering nurture, setting limits, providing incentives for growing up, or serving as a pattern for identification. It is true that, during short periods of regression by the client, the caseworker may need to return to one of these roles temporarily. The caseworker's task, however, is to help the client understand what took place along the road he has traveled and what kind of person he is as a result of these experiences. The client then can develop a picture of the kind of person he is or may become if his misconceptions are cleared away.

IX. General Casework Considerations

WE SHOULD LIKE now to discuss some general considerations about treatment of persons with character disorders. Among the points we shall cover are: the place of the father in the treatment plan; family interaction; psychotic attitudes; the transfer of cases; the special problems inherent in treating these clients in certain settings; and the need for agency co-operation. We shall also comment on the desired qualifications for caseworkers who undertake to treat clients with character disorders and on some aspects of supervision and administration as they affect treatment.

Treatment of Fathers

Although we have a strong conviction that every effort should be made to include fathers in the treatment process, our case illustrations do not give evidence of this conviction. There are several reasons for our overemphasis on the treatment of the mothers. One reason is that the material that seemed most suitable for illustration —particularly the long contact with Mrs. Tenney—happened to deal with women. Another factor that entered into the selection of illustrative cases was the amount of material available in the record. We limited the selection of clinic cases to those handled by the research unit, since these were recorded in greater detail. Another factor affecting the selection of cases was the preponderance of women in treatment in the research unit. In nearly half our cases, the family was without a father because of his death, desertion, or divorce and remarriage. We had contact with several

153

fathers who were at home, but usually they were seen less frequently than were the mothers; in three cases of widowers, the entire contact was with the father. In all instances where a father or stepfather was currently on the scene, we made efforts to see him during the diagnostic study. We were successful in all but a few cases. It is likely that some of these men might have been seen at home in the evening, but the practical problem of travel and of scheduling the caseworkers' time limited the amount of home visiting.

The mother's need to control and to exclude the father from participating in treatment was undoubtedly one factor that influenced some of the men to place responsibility for clinic contact on their wives. We do not believe, however, that the woman's need to be in control was the primary deterrent. In many of these cases the failure of the fathers to participate was only another symptom of the generally deteriorated marital relationship.

In a few cases the father came once but refused to take part in continued treatment. One such refusal was by a man who, in one interview, revealed the depth of his disturbance and the rigidity of the defenses he had erected against a feared psychosis. Several men said they would be willing to continue contacts but were unable to make appointments because they were "too busy." They, too, doubtless had need to defend themselves against involvement.

From our experience we have concluded that the same diagnostic criteria and the same general techniques apply to the treatment of men and women who have character disorders.

Family Interaction

When both the father and mother are in treatment, a great deal can be learned about family interaction and family balance. In one case it became clear that the father's failure to keep appointments, and his interference with the mother's contact by unduly playing up her illness, stemmed from his fear that the clinic would interfere with his domination of the family. This father, like several others under study, suspected that the mother was fostering the rebellion of the adolescent girl against him, although it was obvious to the worker that he was usurping the mother's role with the girl. Unless some of the anxieties of these controlling fathers can be dealt with, they succeed in disrupting the treatment of the child

154

and the mother. Usually there are advantages in having the same worker see both father and mother, particularly in the early contacts, when one parent may have a tendency to be overcontrolling or when they are in competition for the maternal role. Often it is desirable to see them together for a time, or at least occasionally.

When the caseworker observes changes in family balance, he should endeavor to respond to the changing needs of the individuals. For instance, one parent may tend to become depressed and to resort to his usual defensive behavior when the other parent is active or aggressive. Since such interaction can be anticipated, efforts should be made to help the depressed person at a time when he is reacting to the other's increased aggression. The depressed partner at this point needs some special attention which will convey the worker's recognition of the client's special needs associated with the manifest depression; the worker may convey his understanding by giving the client extra time or by clarification.

In the same way, it is often possible to anticipate a shift in behavior on the part of the children in a family. Sometimes, as one child's delinquency begins to improve, another child may begin to act out. In the early stages of treatment, when help is given largely through the relationship itself, the caseworker may only be able to minimize the parent's tendency to shift his own pathology from one child to another. Later, as the parent has less need for such acting-out behavior as a defense, he will be more ready and able to see what is happening to his children.

At the clinic we found that there was value in having periodic conferences at which both parents of the child and all the therapists were present. Obviously the child's therapist had to tell the child about this conference some time in advance and deal with the anxiety that such a concentration of parental figures would stir up. Often it was decided that it was advisable for the child's therapist to be present for only part of the session so that there would not be too much dilution of each parent's relationship with his own therapist or interruption of the process of establishing separate identities for parents and child. The conference provided opportunity for the parents to correct, through reality experience, their fantasies about the other therapists and to gain a sense that they and the clinic staff were all working together.

Psychotic Attitudes

The presence of psychotic attitudes must be regarded as an unfavorable prognosis for treatment of the type we have described. Clinically, many persons with these attitudes fall in the classification of acting-out psychotics rather than of character disorders. They are basically mistrustful of others and therefore cannot identify with persons or incorporate new attitudes. In their early development they came to regard food as poisonous and feeding as dangerous. They have a special kind of pathological sense of identity which is threatened by a close relationship with another person. Treatment of these persons requires different techniques from those that are appropriate for persons with character disorders. The dynamics of these acting-out psychotics and the related treatment implications have been reported on by members of our research unit on childhood schizophrenia.[1]

In the Nye case, it became clear that both parents had such deeply intrenched psychotic attitudes that continued treatment would require the use of the special techniques referred to above. These attitudes were sharply revealed in the interaction between the couple. Mr. N made the original contact after some stealing at home and rebellious behavior on the part of their 14-year-old daughter, Sally. He accepted the plan for treatment on a regular basis, but soon proceeded to try to control the therapist in a provocative way. He belittled his wife and daughter, and said he had embarked on a "new deal." He planned to handle Sally with "understanding" but he intended to be more firm and efficient. Mrs. N reacted to the contact with the clinic by becoming competitive with Sally's therapist. In her interviews with the caseworker she gave long recitals of her activities to prove that she was a good and understanding mother. Later she complained that the case-

[1] Irving Kaufman, M.D., Eleanor Rosenblum, M.S.S., Lora Heims, Ph.D., and Lee Willer, M.D., "Childhood Schizophrenia: Treatment of Children and Parents," *American Journal of Orthopsychiatry*, Vol. XXVII, No. 4 (1957), pp. 683–690.

Irving Kaufman, M.D., Thomas Frank, M.D., Lora Heims, Ph.D., Joan Herrick, M.S.S., and Lee Willer, M.D., "Four Types of Defense in Mothers and Fathers of Schizophrenic Children: Implications for a New Approach to Treatment," *American Journal of Orthopsychiatry*, Vol. XXIX, No. 3 (1959), pp. 460–472.

156

worker never told her anything or answered her questions; in reality, the interviews were marked by an absence of questions on her part and the lack of opportunity for the worker to say anything. It was soon evident that Mrs. N felt that, since she had no access to the therapists of her husband and daughter, they were all talking about her behind her back. The clinic contact obviously had stirred up feelings of being "left out" or "unwanted."

Mrs. N manifested three sets of attitudes. The first was characterized by denial of unpleasant facts; she pretended that the family was a united one and she described herself and her husband as compatible, saying that they agreed about everything. She also stressed her closeness to Sally and her husband, often remarking, "We are one." Her approach to the caseworker was that of a child saying, "See what a good girl I am." Another set of attitudes was marked by extreme dependence. Mrs. N turned over to her husband all the responsibility for Sally and, in doing so, fostered a seductive relationship between them. When Mrs. N had thus succeeded in turning her husband and daughter over to each other, she expressed her deep unfulfilled dependence by talking to the caseworker about her mother and father and her deprivations by them. Mrs. N then reacted to the closeness of the dependent relationship by flight; she developed illness and also tended to withdraw from contact, often missing appointments. She rationalized her broken appointments by telling of her visits to doctors or of engaging in recreational activities with her younger children. In her comments she implied that her duty was to the other children since Sally was as good as dead. During such periods of withdrawal Mrs. N struggled with her husband and Sally for the maternal role. Finally, after Sally had become involved in a sexual episode, clearly precipitated by the father, Mrs. N raised no protest about her husband's withdrawing the whole family from treatment, appearing to submit passively although she gave the impression that she might like to hold on to the caseworker. It is in this kind of situation that the special techniques developed for work with the psychotic are required; the aim is to try to stem the destructive tide of their helpless but omnipotent testing out.

The psychotic attitudes manifested by Mr. and Mrs. N suggest that in their development both were fixated at a more regressed point in the anal continuum than would be found in most character disorders. The caseworker's impression that Mrs. N could not tolerate a close relationship was confirmed by Sally who reported that her mother made no lasting friendships.

In two other cases in our research unit, the mothers exhibited similar fear of involvement which interfered with the establishment of a treatment relationship. One of these mothers maintained contact for a time, but only because her husband insisted on it; she seemed better able to tolerate the closeness of the contact if she did some sort of needlework during the interview. The only time this woman showed any real feeling was after a neighbor, with whom she had sometimes gone shopping, had moved away. She said that although they had never discussed personal matters or visited each other, she missed her. One of the other women presented considerable psychotic material; she had had three earlier admissions to mental hospitals.

It is sometimes difficult to distinguish between psychotic attitudes and the less pervasive mistrust and suspicion that are typical of persons with character disorders. Sometimes considerable observation and testing is required before a differential diagnosis can be made. It is our general observation that parents who are closest to the psychotic end of the continuum are the ones who most frequently require authoritative interference for the protection of the child.

Transfer of Cases

The transfer of cases within an agency always presents problems. The departure of a worker is particularly disturbing to a client who has been traumatized by early loss and who has need throughout life to repeat the experience of the loss. The termination of contact re-emphasizes his old fear of closeness and confirms the conviction that he himself is so unlovable that no one will stay with him. It is important, therefore, to prepare the client as far in advance as possible for the change of workers. The preparation for transfer of these clients should not follow the usual pattern of encouraging them to express anger about the impending loss. Their problem is not that of anger that they are afraid to face; it is, rather, fear that the destructive force of their ever-present anger drives people away. These clients become depressed because of their sense of helplessness and futility. As one woman said, "I had the feeling that all was lost and that I had gone through all this for nothing." What she had "gone through" was the fearful process of learning to trust someone.

The important aspect of the preparation for transfer, therefore, is to help the client see how far he has gone in his development and how much more able he now is to work on his problems. The caseworker should not place emphasis on the sense of loss the client will feel, but should focus on the contact itself, calling special attention to the difficult and negative periods. Reviewing the negatives may serve to avoid the client's tendency to cast the worker, after termination of contact, in the role of the idealized lost mother and to cast the new worker in the role of the bad mother. If the client recognizes that he has coped with certain losses and stresses, he may gain a sense of his ability to live through other difficult times. Even though the client may actually repress some of the things the worker says, he should be helped, as far as possible, to see that the transfer does not mean he must "begin all over again" but that he can proceed from where he is now.

The client may express a wish for the worker's address "so that I can send you a card now and then." The request should usually be granted. The client's purpose in making the request is twofold: to test out the worker to see if he is really being rejected again and to attempt to keep the worker from disappearing into the limbo of lost people. The client probably will use the address rarely, if at all, but his freedom to report progress to the worker can itself be an incentive for change.

The new worker may have to reach out to the client, showing his interest in some tangible way. He should be prepared for regressions, demands, and testing out on the part of the client. Attempts should be made to help the client discuss his feelings about the loss of the previous worker. He may express little feeling, but it is important for the new worker to recognize with the client that the latter has suffered a real loss. The worker should emphasize that grief is what people feel at such a time and that the client's attachment to the former worker is not an affront to the present one. In a surprisingly short time the client is likely not to distinguish between the present worker and his predecessor and will credit the former for many of the latter worker's words and actions. Many clients achieve a transference to the agency itself, saying such things as, "All you people understand these things."

Some of the orally deprived mothers make the transfer difficult by withdrawing at the first news of the impending departure of a worker. They desert before they are deserted. Efforts should be made to get them to return for an interview, preferably by the worker before he leaves. In any event, the withdrawal of the client should not lead to closing the case; the new worker should make a persistent effort to get the client back into contact. Some clients with anal character disorders may continue to deny the fact that the worker is about to leave. In such instances, special effort should be made to talk about the history of the present contact as preparation for a new one.

The countertransference reactions of the new caseworker may also create problems. It is not unusual for a new worker to feel that the former worker indulged the client unnecessarily and that it is up to the new worker to discipline the client. The situation is somewhat analogous to that of a foster mother who decides that the parents have "spoiled" a child. The client who has lost a supporting relationship regresses, and his regressive behavior serves to substantiate the new worker's negative appraisal. Since the client with a character disorder is peculiarly sensitive to attitudes about giving and withholding, the worker's negative feelings may precipitate a hopeless struggle between them which can only be resolved by another transfer.

The Setting

Parents with character disorders are clients of many community services. In general, they present the same therapeutic problems in any setting, but they also present some particular problems in particular agencies.

Family service agencies have always had a relatively large number of persons with character disorders in their caseloads. In recent years, as knowledge about their dynamics has become more clearly formulated, agencies have endeavored to develop techniques appropriate to their needs. In earlier periods many of these clients dropped contact after one or two abortive attempts by the worker to establish a relationship. They often were helped with practical problems on a recurrent or "brief-service" basis.

It is also true that family service agencies, traditionally, have carried a number of cases of character disorders on a long-time basis. The clients in this group often seek help from these agencies because of difficulties in their social and personal relationships, such as marital conflict, behavior problems of children, and illegitimate pregnancy. As family caseworkers have gained fuller understanding of the dynamics involved in such acting-out behavior, they have developed skill in involving these clients in a meaningful relationship and in furthering their psychological growth.

Even if these clients turn to family agencies for only occasional help, it seems likely that the service given is not without meaning to them. A client may have contact with the agency only once in six months or a year, but it seems likely that, in his mind, the case is never "closed." The fact that he knows there is an agency to which he can turn is itself a sustaining force. He endows the agency with the parental power and omnipotence which he finds necessary for someone to have. The help given to such clients in seemingly random contacts may, in aggregate, dispel part of their basic fear and distrust of people. Obviously, many of these clients would derive greater benefit from sustained treatment. However, when agency resources do not permit sustained service, maximum use should be made of intermittent contacts because of their dynamic meaning to the client.

Medical social workers are also frequently involved with persons with character disorders. Because of the high incidence of physical symptoms in this group and because of their lack of inner and outer resources to deal with them, these clients put heavy demands on medical resources. Greater attention has been focused on them in recent years as psychosomatic medicine has come to recognize the immature core in the personality of this type of patient. When medical social workers endeavor to refer these clients to other agencies for continued care, difficulties are encountered because of the clients' reactions. Such a client may develop separation anxiety or somatic symptoms which must be dealt with before

161

he is able to move on. Since financial need is frequently involved, the question of division of responsibility between a medical social service and other community agencies arises. It is perhaps safe to say that whenever two or more agencies disagree strongly about responsibility for a case, the client probably has a character disorder.

Child placement agencies, both public and private, also have under their care a large percentage of parents with character disorders. If the placement plan is based on the assumption that the child will be returned to his family, it is essential that some agency take responsibility for continued treatment of the family. Who is to carry this responsibility is another matter. In some cases it may be the child-placing agency itself; in others, the primary responsibility may be taken by a public welfare department, a probation or protective service, or a family service agency.

Agencies dealing with unmarried parents are also familiar with this group of clients. The unmarried mother often can profit by a period of sustained treatment, whether she places the baby for adoption, uses a foster home facility, or keeps the baby with her. In general, the caseworker who has had contact with the girl during the pregnancy has the best chance of maintaining a relationship with her through the crucial period thereafter. It is of utmost importance to provide help at this time because of the significance of a baby to a woman with a character disorder. Without help, the mother will establish a pathological relationship with the child if she keeps him; if she places him, she is likely to repeat her acting-out behavior. Histories of mothers of delinquents underline the fact that this period is an extremely crucial one.

Courts and other protective agencies, as well as public welfare agencies, have a particular need to understand the dynamics of persons with character disorders. These agencies, more than others, represent the authority of the community. Contrary to widespread belief, authority in itself is not distasteful to persons with character disorders. In reality, these persons long for control but it must have one essential requirement—it must represent the authority of the loving parent. Erich Fromm points out that there is general confusion in regard to the concept of authority: ". . . it is widely believed that we are confronted with the alternative of having

162

dictatorial, irrational authority or of having no authority at all." [2]
He describes "rational authority" as that kind which has its source
in competence and is used in helping rather than exploiting. In
a later book he states, "In the rational kind of authority, the strength
of the emotional ties tends to *decrease* in direct proportion to the
degree to which the person subjected to the authority becomes
stronger and thereby more similar to the authority." [3] Elliot Studt
has expressed similar views: "On the basis of our knowledge of human growth we readily accept the principle that authority in the
sense of loving, effective participation by the more mature and
responsible individual in the decisions of the less mature is essential
at all stages of development, particularly in the early formative
stages and in times of unusual stress." [4]

Public assistance agencies represent a form of authority which can
often be used constructively with these immature clients. There
has been an increasing trend in the public welfare field to provide
the type of relationship and the special services needed by such
families. The caseworker in these agencies is in a particularly
strategic position to play the role of a person in authority who has
concern about the individual's welfare, and who is in a position
to provide needed resources and services.

Courts and protective agencies usually deal with persons who are
not voluntarily seeking help. [5] In recent years, both probation
officers and persons attached to voluntary protective agencies have
stressed the necessity for establishing a positive working relationship
with families that come under their supervision. These workers
should understand the degree of ego weakness present in the parents
of these families if they are to provide them with the authoritative
support they need and often want. Under the supervision of a
court or a protective agency, families often maintain a good level
of functioning, only to relapse into difficulty if such supervision is
withdrawn prematurely.

[2] Erich Fromm, M.D., *Man for Himself,* Rinehart and Co., New York, 1947,
p. 9.
[3] Erich Fromm, M.D., *The Sane Society,* Rinehart and Co., New York, 1955,
p. 97.
[4] Elliot Studt, "An Outline for Study of Social Authority Factors in Casework,"
Social Casework, Vol. XXXV, No. 6 (1954), p. 235.
[5] Irving Kaufman, M.D., "The Contribution of Protective Services," *Child
Welfare,* Vol. XXXVI, No. 2 (1957), pp. 8–12.

Co-operative Efforts

Families whose members have character disorders may require a battery of services rather than the help of one person. Unfortunately, such co-operative work has been the exception rather than the rule. A number of factors are responsible for the resistance of agencies and workers to entering wholeheartedly into co-operative plans. Sometimes agencies have been fearful about unnecessary duplication of service. Sometimes they have been uneasy about discussing confidential material. Or they may have questions about the advisability of diluting an existing therapeutic relationship.

There is evidence that barriers are beginning to give way and that agencies are working more closely together, both in dealing with individual cases and in establishing various kinds of joint projects. Such co-operation, in the interest of persons with character disorders, is more likely to flourish if the various agencies concerned operate on a common theoretical base and if they all recognize the importance of sustained service for these families.

Obviously, appropriate procedures and division of work must be agreed upon. Confidentiality must be respected but distinctions should be made between real confidences and information that is community knowledge. In considering the matter of the therapeutic relationship with a particular worker, one must remember that these clients have the capacity to relate to more than one person. As we have indicated earlier, they are often able to make use of several helping persons at one time because of their diffuse sense of parental identity. Once agencies have agreed upon an over-all approach, the workers can often move ahead quite independently, each contributing to the family's growth and stability.

Qualifications of Caseworkers

Caseworkers who undertake to treat clients with character disorders must not only be professionally qualified but must be temperamentally suited for the job. As must be abundantly clear by now, the treatment task places tremendous intellectual and emotional demands on persons who undertake to treat these clients. Although one relates to them in an emotional rather than an intellectual way, intellectual understanding of what is taking place is essential at every step in treatment. Obviously, the casework should be based on sound knowledge of psychodynamics and psychopathology, and understanding of differentiations between character disorders, neuroses, and psychoses. Too often in the past, clients with character disorders were not properly identified by psychiatrists and caseworkers and, as a result, the behavior of these clients baffled and disturbed the persons who were endeavoring to help them. Considerable experience is needed before one becomes adept in understanding the meaning of the symbolic acting-out behavior of these clients and even the manifest content of what they say.

During their training period, caseworkers have less opportunity than have psychiatrists and clinical psychologists to study and observe the dynamics of this or any other clinical syndrome. Caseworkers, of course, have many other subject areas to master. Also, the teaching of psychodynamics is generally oriented to the casework task, which is not primarily that of dealing with unconscious phenomena. In treating persons with character disorders, however, one is directly involved with primitive, unrepressed expressions of the unconscious. The casework task, obviously, is not to interpret the meaning of the manifestations. The caseworker, however, must find ways of communicating with the unrepressed libidinal and aggressive impulses which are so much a part of the client's daily life. Extensive experience and considerable clinical study are usually required before caseworkers are able to recognize, understand, and respond appropriately to these expressions of unconscious impulses.

The caseworker, therefore, should be a person who is able to communicate verbally and nonverbally with people whose behavior is often bizarre and asocial and whose attitudes in the relationship are aggressive, childish, and provocative. In order to do this, the caseworker must be constantly alert to his own feelings. Suppression of feeling will not be helpful, since fluidity of feeling is necessary for nonverbal communication. The worker's expression of feeling must at all times be genuine, since these clients have a kind of paranoid sensitivity to "phony" or assumed attitudes. At certain times the caseworker must express his own opinions with a directness that would not be appropriate in the treatment of a neurotic. At other times he may need to exert considerable control to avoid

165

expressing his feelings of anger or disapproval; such control itself is a vehicle for transmitting acceptance and understanding.

In working with these clients, the caseworker must endeavor to be aware of his own impulses and fantasies. He must be able to control his own delinquent impulses and identifications but, at the same time, he must be able to identify with delinquent behavior to the extent of understanding it. If caseworkers and other persons who deal with delinquents do not have considerable self-awareness, they may seek vicarious gratification from the activities of their clients or take pleasure in the punishment that these activities call forth. Sometimes they get satisfaction from both the activity and the punishment, as certain parents do who first stimulate acting-out by the child and then play the role of a punishing parent. Needless to say, these characteristics constitute a severe handicap for anyone working with persons with character disorders.

Certain fantasies about the client's needs may also constitute pitfalls for the unwary caseworker. One common fantasy is that the child is the victim of his parents' neglect and that the caseworker must come to his rescue. If the caseworker acts on the fantasy, he estranges the parents by confirming their expectation that they will be blamed and misunderstood. Also, the caseworker himself is likely to suffer disappointment since the child, more often than not, soon reveals his attachment to his parents and his lack of interest in being rescued. Another fantasy that a caseworker may develop is that he can be an all-loving parent to the adult client who suffered many deprivations as a child and who has been searching all his life for someone to play this role. In such instances the caseworker, like the inexperienced foster parent, is unprepared for the negative reactions of the client—his testing of limits, his excessive demands, his efforts to provoke rejection or abandonment, and his withdrawal or other characteristic protection against hurt.

The caseworker obviously must have ability to identify readily with these confused clients but, at the same time, he must have a sure sense of his own identity. He need not relate to the client in a static way; rather, he should be able to manifest his inner strengths in his ability to question and consider issues and to act on his convictions. He should be warm without being seductive and firm without being punitive. He should be able to accept the feelings

166

of his clients without having to identify with their ways of acting. He must learn to meet them on their own ground and to communicate readily with them regardless of their economic or social status.

Attention has been called in recent years to the differences in values and attitudes between caseworkers and certain groups of clients. It has been pointed out that the "middle-class" values of the former constitute a barrier to understanding the "lower-class" values of "hard-to-reach" clients. Two factors should be considered in connection with this matter. The obvious one is that not all "hard-to-reach" clients fall into the lower social and economic groups. These clients may be salesmen, physicists, or housewives with a good social background. Another factor, often overlooked, is that the barriers to communication may lie in the area of psychosexual values as much as in the area of cultural values. Adults are often intolerant of others whose behavior indicates a lower level of development, in the same way that a child who has recently been toilet trained is scornful of younger children who still wet themselves. Much of the indignation about the "outrageous" behavior of persons with character disorders has something of this flavor about it and may stem from uneasiness about the mastery of primitive impulses. It is understandable that social workers, as well as others endeavoring to work with these relatively immature persons, often react with indignation when a client sleeps until noon, squanders the rent money, or goes on an alcoholic binge. Such behavior is an affront to one's standards, both cultural and psychosocial. If the differences in standards are understood by the person endeavoring to help others, his own self-awareness will help reduce the barriers between him and those who may have a different orientation toward life.

Supervisory and Agency Support

The caseworker who undertakes to treat the impulse-ridden client who has a severe character disorder needs the support of his agency. The supervisor is usually the key person to provide such support and guidance. The relatively inexperienced worker needs the opportunity to discuss his reactions to the client, as well as the benefit of the supervisor's wider knowledge and experience. Even more experienced caseworkers should have an opportunity for consultation, since clients of this group have such a strong emotional impact on anyone who deals with them. There are many times when the caseworker urgently needs someone to listen to him with a sympathetic ear. The supervisor, in order to be of maximum help, should have sufficient experience to be able to give the worker reality-oriented advice and to stimulate analysis of the meaning of the client's puzzling behavior. Of particular importance is the supervisor's skill in recognizing the caseworker's inevitable emotional reactions. These treatment-facilitating functions can sometimes be performed by members of a working team or staff unit.

Another important agency responsibility, whether carried by the supervisor or a team director, is to create an atmosphere in which the caseworker can develop his skill, particularly his intuition. Intuition is a subtle quality that each person must develop for himself, but the development can be encouraged and stimulated if it is sufficiently valued by leaders in the agency. Intuition, basically, is a combination of ready identification with another person and responsiveness to his communications. It is the ability to look beyond a literal interpretation of words or actions and to sense the underlying meaning. In supervision, the caseworker's feelings or hunches should be explored sufficiently to reveal their bases. Through such exploration, the caseworker learns to distinguish between feelings that are the result of his sensitive receptivity to communication from the client and those that are merely projections of his own attitudes or biases. The ability to distinguish between the two, especially in working with this group of clients, is one mark of skill. A supervisor may not be able to help all caseworkers make such distinctions, but he has responsibility to determine the extent of the caseworker's subjective responses. If a worker tends to rely too heavily on his intuitive ability or on his natural ease in making superficial relationships, the supervisor should try to stimulate him to acquire more technical knowledge. Too many promising workers fail to develop skill because they rely entirely on their intuitions.

Often the skill of a caseworker can be enhanced if the supervisor encourages him to engage in some experimentation with the understanding that careful attention will be given to the results. Obviously, the worker should be helped to analyze both successes and failures. His experimentation should not be wildly individualistic nor should it be carried out so rigidly as to create anxiety.

Successful supervision can take place only if the relationship is based on mutual respect on the part of supervisor and supervisee— a respect that permits each to make an honest appraisal of the qualifications of the other. A supervisor should be able to face the fact that some workers may have acquired certain skills which he himself does not possess or have made greater advances in a certain direction than he has. The fact that a worker has special skills does not mean that the supervisor can no longer be of help to him. Supervision encompasses much more than teaching, and workers of all levels of experience need some form of help and direction. For workers with considerable experience, the relationship between the two persons may more properly be termed "consultation."

Both the casework and the supervisory staff will be handicapped in working with this group of clients if they do not have the wholehearted support of the administrative staff and the board. The understanding of clients with character disorders cannot be limited to those involved in the treatment program but must pervade the total agency. Unless the caseworker has the support of the executive and board members, who must also understand why progress is slow and why results can be accomplished only by long-term treatment, he will be subject to continual pressure to act against the interest of the client; he may be asked to close certain cases arbitrarily, to cut relief, or to urge clients to take certain actions that can only end in failure or in their further regression. An administrator who does not have thorough understanding of this group of clients may unwittingly adopt policies or enter into interagency agreements that will hinder the treatment program.

The administrator, as well as the staff members engaged in practice, has responsibility to interpret the needs of these troubled clients, not only to the board members or other sponsors of the agency program but to the public generally. All members of the staff need rather extensive knowledge about the dynamics of these clients. They also must have considerable conviction about the client's potential for change, if they are to interpret a treatment program effectively.

169

X. The Challenge

NOTHING SHORT OF A general community approach will be effective in reducing the widespread problems of juvenile delinquency and other forms of serious personal and family pathology. Isolated efforts, unrelated to a general treatment approach, are likely to lose a great deal of their potential value. These community problems must be viewed in their entirety, with recognition of their social and their characterological aspects, if they are to be truly understood and brought under control.

Obviously, there is necessity to improve the social conditions that play a large part in creating the pathology. Efforts must be continued to improve housing and public assistance standards, and to develop adequate resources for health care, vocational training, recreation, and so forth. It is unlikely, however, that these efforts will be effective in reducing the widespread social pathology unless they take into account the characterological aspects of the problem. In general, the characterological aspects of delinquency and family disorganization are not clearly understood. It is important for sound community planning that the interconnection between social and psychological factors, both in etiology and in treatment, be more fully taken into account.

For example, if we look closely at the problem of poor housing we can see some of these interconnections. The fact that large numbers of people with character disorders live in slum areas is not accidental. Not only do slums spread a kind of contagion and tend to reinforce pathological tendencies, but cheap housing itself

170

operates as a selective factor in determining which families live in a particular neighborhood or dwelling. Poor housing and blighted neighborhoods become the receiving ground for persons who are at the bottom of the economic scale and who, in the main, are in this position because of personality difficulties. They are persons who have little success in work and who have had criminal records or a history of family desertion, illegitimacy, alcoholism, and so forth. In other words, many of them have serious character disorders which have interfered with their success in work, marriage, and other aspects of social functioning. A slum neighborhood attracts them not only because the rents are low and the landlords are "not fussy" about references, but because it provides them with a background of general dilapidation which fits into their image of themselves. The need for these people to be "dilapidated," like many of their other characteristics, is difficult for the average person to believe or understand. As one works closely with this group of clients, however, one comes to sense that this psychological need plays a large part in determining where they choose to live.

In one instance, a social agency helped a family that lived in a rundown house in a particularly poor neighborhood of stores and rooming houses to move to better quarters, only to find that the family had moved back to the old place in less than a year. The mother explained that she felt more comfortable in the old neighborhood. Another mother whose husband had been imprisoned for incest with their young daughter moved immediately after his imprisonment from a good residential neighborhood to a slum. It was clear that she felt so degraded by what had happened that she felt she did not deserve a decent home. Although she complained about the neighborhood and was afraid to let the children play on the street, she was apathetic to efforts of her minister to find her a better place to live. She could not accept the offer of better housing until she was helped to feel less depreciated and, hence, to develop a different self-image.

During periods of acute housing shortage, families often must live in undesirable neighborhoods. This was true during World War II. As soon as better housing became available, however, large numbers of families moved to the new apartments and housing developments. Often their economic situation was then improved

171

because of the employment of the wife or older children. The families who remained in the slum areas were mostly those with fewer resources, both economic and emotional; when the children reached adolescence, they usually brought additional problems rather than additional income to the family. During and after the depression of the thirties, a similar process took place; many families moved to cheaper housing, but those with strength were able to re-establish themselves economically when jobs became available and to find more desirable living quarters. A poor neighborhood will often be inhabited temporarily by the latest migrants from other countries or from rural areas in this country. In a few years, however, most of the better organized families move on, leaving behind those with various types of problems or limitations.

These illustrations of the issues involved in poor housing are presented to highlight the relationship between the pathology of persons with character disorders and social phenomena. If the characterological aspects were more generally understood, remedial measures could be devised which would be more in keeping with the psychological defenses of these people. There are some encouraging signs in this direction, such as studies being made of the attitudes of families who are being uprooted by large urban renewal projects [1] and efforts to bring advanced social work thinking to bear on the problems of tenants in low-cost housing. An experimental project, at LaGuardia Houses in New York City, has been described.[2] In another article [3] Drayton S. Bryant has pointed out that if the workers in the fields of housing, community organization, group work, and casework can successfully integrate their efforts, as has been done in a few instances, great strides can be made toward the creation of a "feeling of community" among the tenants. Such an approach may be found to be particularly helpful with disorganized families. The same principles may be successfully applied to private housing developments or even to certain neighborhoods or city blocks.

[1] Herbert J. Gans, "The Human Implications of Current Redevelopment and Relocation Planning," *Journal of the American Institute of Planners,* Vol. XXV, No. 1 (1959), pp. 15–25.

[2] Murray E. Ortof, "Public Housing: New Neighbors in Old Communities," *Social Work,* Vol. IV, No. 2 (1959), pp. 55–63.

[3] Drayton S. Bryant, "The Next Twenty Years in Public Housing," *Social Work,* Vol. IV, No. 2 (1959), pp. 46–54.

Our discussion of the relation of disorganized families to city housing problems may suggest that families with character disorders are to be found only in metropolitan areas. No such implication is intended. Persons who work in rural areas must deal with similar problems of pathology and sometimes with even more serious lacks of housing and other health and social resources. The social worker in small towns and rural areas frequently must exercise considerable ingenuity in order to find effective ways of providing appropriate services for these families, whether they are found in the "Tobacco Roads" of the South or in the tarpaper shacks of northern New England.

New Approaches

In order to attack a community's problems of social pathology effectively, there should be co-ordination of various health and welfare services. These services need not be in a single administrative unit; nevertheless, persons working in each program should be aware of the part their efforts play in a larger whole.

At the present time, existing social agencies usually have contact with these troubled families only at times of crisis or breakdown, such as delinquency of children, need for placement of children, economic problems, severe illness, marital conflict, and so forth. One approach might be to provide supervision to such families in relation to the normal tension points—marriage, childbirth, child's entrance in school, occupational choice, and so forth.[4] A number of religious groups already do a great deal of family visiting on a regular basis and these visitors are available to families when a crisis occurs. Such preventive work is particularly valuable for persons with character disorders. In spite of their nonconforming behavior, many maintain an active church connection. Many others would like such an affiliation if they were sure of being welcomed and of not being made to feel even more sinful and inferior.

[4] Erich Lindemann, Warren T. Vaughan, and Manon McGinnis, "Preventive Intervention in a Four-year-old Child whose Father Committed Suicide," *Emotional Problems of Early Childhood*, Gerald Caplan, M.D. (ed.), Basic Books, New York, 1955, pp. 5–30.

173

Group therapy and other group processes have been used effectively by agencies dealing with delinquents and their families.[5] A group experience has special meaning to persons with character disorders, since they feel great loneliness as a result of their fear of close relationships. One orally deprived mother who was chronically depressed told with sudden enthusiasm about her membership in a new club that had been formed by the waitress in a local diner. She explained that the club's activities included "sewing, not swearing, and going to nightclubs." The money for the visits to nightclubs was raised by fines imposed on the members for swearing or forgetting to bring their sewing. (None of them liked to sew.) When the club disbanded for the summer, this mother felt genuinely bereaved. In other groups she had briefly attended—including a church group where she had been treated very kindly—she had felt hopelessly inferior. These immature women cannot be expected to take an active part in the usual community groups.

In the adaptation of group work techniques to meet the needs of persons having character disorders, the modifications, like those made in casework techniques, should be based on these clients' defenses and on the underlying meaning of their behavior. Some of the principles and techniques of group therapy with delinquent adolescent girls have been reported by members of our research unit.[6] The principles are equally applicable to similar work with mothers, especially women who utilize activity or denial as a defense against their depression.

In the report mentioned above, special attention was called to the following points: (1) The membership of a group should not have great variance in age, intelligence, or economic status, since marked differences reinforce the types of resistance these clients tend to use. (2) The leader must first enter the defense structure of the group in order to become part of it; only then is it possible to effect therapeutic change. (3) Questions about feelings should

[5] Harris B. Peck, M.D. and Virginia Bellsmith, *Treatment of the Delinquent Adolescent: Group and Individual Therapy with Parent and Child,* Family Service Association of America, New York, 1954.

[6] Alice Fleming, M.D. and Irving Kaufman, M.D., "Training for Group Therapy with Adolescent Delinquent Girls." Paper presented at a meeting of the American Orthopsychiatric Association in Chicago, March, 1957. Unpublished.

174

be avoided for some time. (4) Requests for concrete information should be answered directly without attempts to clarify the underlying feelings. (5) The tendency of members to use the group to act out separation and desertion anxiety must be dealt with directly. The leader should take a positive stand about attendance, inquiring about and contacting absent members; this activity cannot be left to the other members, as can be done with some groups. The absent member requires direct communication from the leader, and the other members will watch to see whether it is forthcoming. Since the other members tend to react to loss by a protective use of denial, their lack of regret when a member has dropped out cannot be taken literally. The leader's attitude and activity in relation to the absent one have meaning to them for they sense that he would also look for them if they were absent.

Therapeutic or educational groups organized for persons with character disorders must offer more than one inducement for attendance; the program should include a variety of activities even though the main focus is to discuss a common interest, such as housekeeping or bringing up children. The discussion period should be relatively short and time should always be reserved for refreshments and general sociability. One such group of mothers met in a small public library while their preschool children attended a story hour. The group was under the sponsorship of a family service agency as part of its family life education program. Originally the group had been organized by a few active women who had arranged for the leader, carried responsibility for planning, and had taken the chief part in the discussions. Soon these active women moved away from the neighborhood. The remaining eight were shy and retiring, and had participated little in the discussions; they all had suffered considerable social deprivation. However, they showed interest in having the group continue, and after some initial awkwardness they began to talk more freely. They resisted the idea of a set agenda, preferring to talk spontaneously. They enjoyed serving the coffee and cake, and as each woman took her turn she became more at ease in the group. Often the most significant discussion took place around the coffee table.

The leader found the response of these women different from that of the other groups she had led. They had no tendency to cast her in the role of "expert"; in fact, they rarely asked her opinion but accepted her as one of the group, with a kind of tacit recognition that her presence somehow kept things going. Although the group met only once a month, the mothers showed a noticeable growth over a period of three years in their handling of their children, in their appearance and dress, in their general ease in conversation, and in their self-confidence. These gains seemed to carry over to other situations.

The first year was a period of slow testing. At first the group members could admit they had problems only about very minor and safe issues; the woman reporting the problem would show relief when someone else acknowledged a similar one. It was not until the second year that they began talking about their childhood deprivations. During the third year, they were able to focus on a few specific problems in relation to their children. At the end of this period the group disbanded, largely because several of the women had taken part-time jobs.

Another interesting report of group treatment of "hard-to-reach" mothers, conducted under the auspices of a family agency, has recently been reported by Hanna Grunwald.[7] There seems to be growing evidence that group techniques have great potential for the treatment of both adolescents and parents with character disorders.

It should be noted that group therapy is not a less expensive or a less time-consuming way of helping these clients. As is true of all treatment procedures, there are definite indications and counterindications for its use. It has a special place among the therapeutic tools and has much to offer as a form of direct treatment or as a supplement to individual treatment. In some instances group therapy may be helpful in preparing the client for individual treatment.

Co-ordination of Effort

A co-ordinated community program to help families whose members have character disorders would require that each social agency

[7] Hanna Grunwald, Ph.D., "Group Counseling with the Multiproblem Family," *The Use of Group Techniques in the Family Agency*, Family Service Association of America, New York, 1959, pp. 31–42.

undertake three responsibilities: (1) to improve its own particular services to these families; (2) to make co-operative work with other agencies a fact rather than a vague wish; and (3) to carry on an educational campaign with its board, its constituency, and the public generally. In addition, effort should be made to involve persons from various community services that are not strictly within the social welfare field, such as educators, judges, police officers, and librarians. Preventive services of various kinds should be provided in order to help parents of these families with their responsibilities of child rearing. As the parents come to understand the needs of their children they often achieve a higher degree of maturity themselves.

Not many people will disagree with the goals we have described, but many may ask, "Can we afford the cost?" There is only one answer: The community pays in one way or the other. We all live in the same world and we rise and fall together. Unless persons with character disorders are helped to reach a higher level of maturity, their numbers will be multiplied and public expenditures will increase proportionately.

Bibliography

Abraham, Karl, M.D., "The Influence of Oral Erotism on Character Formation," *Selected Papers on Psychoanalysis,* Hogarth Press, London, 1927, pp. 393–406.

——————, "Contributions to the Theory of the Anal Character," *Selected Papers on Psychoanalysis,* Hogarth Press, London, 1927, pp. 370–392.

Barry, Elizabeth, "Some Problems in Protective Casework Technique: A Case Presentation," in *Ego Psychology and Dynamic Casework,* Howard J. Parad (ed.), Family Service Association of America, New York, 1958, pp. 126–136.

Berman, Sidney, "Antisocial Character Disorder: Its Etiology and Relationship to Delinquency," *American Journal of Orthopsychiatry,* Vol. XXIX, No. 3 (1959), pp. 612–613.

Dick, Kenneth and Strnad, Lydia J., "The Multi-problem Family and Problems of Service," *Social Casework,* Vol. XXXIX, No. 6 (1958), pp. 349–355.

Eissler, K. R., M.D. (ed.), *Searchlights on Delinquency,* International Universities Press, New York, 1949.

Fike, Norma, "Social Treatment of Long-Term Dependency," *Social Work,* Vol. II, No. 4 (1957), pp. 51–56.

Freud, Sigmund, "Character and Anal Erotism," *Collected Papers, Vol. II,* Hogarth Press, London, 4th ed., 1946, pp. 45–50.

——————, "On the Transformation of the Instincts with Special Reference to Anal Erotism," *Collected Papers, Vol. II,* Hogarth Press, London, 4th ed., 1946, pp. 164–171.

——————, "Three Contributions to the Theory of Sex," in *The Basic Writings of Sigmund Freud,* A. A. Brill (ed.), Modern Library, Random House, New York, 1938.

Friedlander, Kate, *The Psycho-analytical Approach to Juvenile Delinquency,* International Universities Press, New York, 1947.

Glover, Edward, "Notes on Oral Character Formation," *International Journal of Psychoanalysis,* Vol. VI, No. 2 (1925), pp. 131–154.

Glueck, Sheldon and Glueck, Eleanor T., *Unravelling Juvenile Delinquency,* Commonwealth Fund, New York, 1950.

Johnson, Adelaide M., M.D. and Szurek, S. A., M.D., "Genesis of Antisocial Acting Out in Children and Adults," *Psychoanalytic Quarterly,* Vol. XXI, No. 3 (1952), pp. 323–343.

Jones, Ernest, "Anal Erotic Character Traits," *Papers on Psychoanalysis,* Williams and Wilkins, Baltimore, 5th ed., 1949, pp. 413–437.

178

Kaufman, Irving, M.D., "Therapeutic Considerations of the Borderline Personality Structure," in *Ego Psychology and Dynamic Casework*, Howard J. Parad (ed.), Family Service Association of America, New York, 1958, pp. 99–110.

————, "Three Basic Sources for Pre-Delinquent Character," *The Nervous Child*, Vol. XI, No. 1 (1955), pp. 12–22.

———— and Heims, Lora, "The Body Image of the Juvenile Delinquent," *American Journal of Orthopsychiatry*, Vol. XXVIII, No. 1 (1958), pp. 146–157.

————, Makkay, Elizabeth S., and Zilbach, Joan, "The Impact of Adolescence on Girls with Delinquent Character Formation," *American Journal of Orthopsychiatry*, Vol. XXIX, No. 1 (1959), pp. 130–143.

Leach, Jean M., "Casework Techniques in the Treatment of Character Disorders," in *Casework Papers, 1956*, Family Service Association of America, New York, 1956, pp. 53–59.

Michaels, Joseph J., *Disorders of Character*, Charles C. Thomas, Springfield, Illinois, 1955.

Peck, Harris B., M.D. and Bellsmith, Virginia, *Treatment of the Delinquent Adolescent*, Family Service Association of America, New York, 1954.

Rexford, Eveoleen N. and van Amerongen, Suzanne Taetz, M.D., "The Influence of Unsolved Maternal Oral Conflicts upon Impulsive Acting Out in Young Children," *American Journal of Orthopsychiatry*, Vol. XXVII, No. 1 (1957), pp. 75–87.

Ruesch, Jurgen, M.D., "The Infantile Personality: The Core Problem of Psychosomatic Medicine," *Psychosomatic Medicine*, Vol. X, No. 3 (1948), pp. 134–144.

Scherz, Frances M., "Treatment of Acting-Out Character Disorders in a Marital Problem," in *Casework Papers, 1956*, Family Service Association of America, New York, 1956, pp. 37–52.

Schmideberg, Melitta, M.D., and Sokol, Jack, "The Function of Contact in Psychotherapy with Offenders," *Social Casework*, Vol. XXXIV, No. 9 (1953), pp. 385–392.

Simcox, Beatrice R. and Kaufman, Irving, M.D., "Handling of Early Contacts with Parents of Delinquents," *Social Casework*, Vol. XXXVII, No. 9 (1956), pp. 443–450.

————, "Treatment of Character Disorders in Parents of Delinquents," *Social Casework*, Vol. XXXVII, No. 8 (1956), pp. 388–395.

Studt, Elliot, "The Contribution of Correctional Practice to Social Work Theory and Education," *Social Casework*, Vol. XXXVII, No. 6 (1956), pp. 263–269.

————, "An Outline for Study of Social Authority Factors in Casework," *Social Casework*, Vol. XXXV, No. 6 (1954), pp. 231–238.

Warren, Effie, "Treatment of Marriage Partners with Character Disorders," *Social Casework*, Vol. XXXVIII, No. 3 (1957), pp. 118–126.